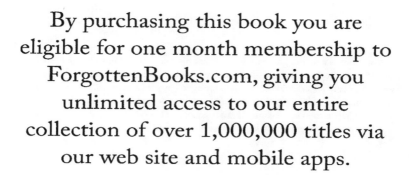

ISBN 978-0-260-53200-8
PIBN 10954444

A Historic Resources Study:
The Civil War Defenses of Washington
Part II

United States Department of Interior
National Park Service
National Capital Region
Washington, DC

Contract No. 144CX300096053

Prepared by
CEHP, Incorporated
Chevy Chase, Maryland

A Historic Resources Study:
The Civil War Defenses of Washington
Part II

United States Department of Interior
National Park Service
National Capital Region
Washington, DC

Contract No. 144CX300096053

Prepared by
CEHP, Incorporated
Chevy Chase, Maryland

A Historic Resources Study:
The Civil War Defenses of Washington
Part II

Table Contents

* Appendices are under separate cover

Chapter I

Silenced Guns

Abandonment of the Fortifications

Following Confederate General Jubal A. Early's Raid on Washington, DC, the threat to the nation's capital diminished considerably. Many units formerly stationed at one of the forts in the Defenses of Washington found themselves in the field, most likely in the Army of the Potomac, and possibly converted from artillery to infantry. No additional Confederate invasions or attacks on the Defenses of Washington occurred.[1]

After the Confederate Army of Northern Virginia's surrender at Appomattox, VA, on April 9, 1865, the Defenses of Washington performed its last military function of the Civil War. In the midst of Washington's exuberant celebrations, "The chain of forts around the city, and batteries of field artillery between, made a ring of cannons around the city which were fired in rotation for several hours. The line of cannon salutes running round and round the other always proceeded in the same direction, so that it went round and round the circuit 20 to 30 miles."[2] But, at the same time, the War Department began planning the reduction of the U.S. Army including its size, activities, property, etc. Soon, the War Department issued General Orders No. 77, "For Reducing Expenses of the Military Establishment," April 28, 1865, that included the following pertinent passages:

> I. That the chiefs of the respective bureaus of this Department proceed immediately to reduce the expenses of their respective departments to what is absolutely necessary, in view of an immediate reduction of the forces in the field and garrison and the speedy termination of hostilities, and that they severally make out statements of the reductions they deem practicable.
>
> V. That the chief engineers stop work on all field fortifications and other works, except those for which specific appropriations have been made by Congress for completion, or that may be required for the proper protection of works in progress.
>
> VII. The Adjutant-General of the Army will cause immediate returns to be made by all commanders in the field, garrisons, detachments, and posts of their respective forces, with a view to their immediate reduction.
>
> VIII. The Quartermaster's, Subsistence, Ordnance, Engineer, and Provost-Marshal-General's departments will reduce the number of clerks and employés to that absolutely required for closing the business of their respective departments, and will without delay report to the Secretary of War the number required of each class or grade: The Surgeon-General will make similar reductions of medical officers, nurses, and attendants in his Bureau.
>
> IX. The chiefs of the respective bureaus will immediately cause property returns to be made out of the public property in their charge, and a statement of the property in each that may be sold upon advertisement and public sale without prejudice to the service.[3]

The Engineer Bureau had already been considering end-of-the-war dispositions and had informed the commanding general of its intentions:

ENGINEER DEPARTMENT,
Washington, April 21, 1865

Brig. Gen. John A. Rawlins,
Chief of Staff, Armies of the United States,
Headquarters General Grant, Washington, D.C.:

GENERAL: I have the honor to recommend to the lieutenant-general that instructions may be given to the generals of departments to confine the labor on temporary fieldworks to such as can be performed by the troops; to avoid all further expenditure in the employment of hired operatives and purchase of material, and to collect and preserve all tools and property appertaining to the engineer service, to the end that they be held for sale or transportation to depots hereafter to be designated, or held ready for immediate use when required; also the same instructions in relation to siege material and bridge trains. The chief engineer has caused property and funds to be forwarded to the engineer officers assigned to duty under the generals commanding in the field, which commanders are the judges of the necessity and expediency of constructing the works of offense and defense, as occasion may require. Hence, the chief engineer cannot with propriety interfere in suspending any of the works in progress, and therefore suggests that the lieutenant-general call the attention of the commanders in such localities as he may see fit to the subject now presented. In every department attention may probably be given at once to the collection of tools, property, and instruments, and great saving of treasure effected by early attention to this subject. It is also recommended that the department commanders require their engineer officers to keep on hand a specified supply of tools, &c., to meet any emergency, forwarding the residue to depots.

Respectfully, your obedient servant,

RICH'D DELAFIELD,
Brigadier-General and Chief Engineer, U.S. Army[4]

And the Engineer Bureau then issued the following circular to all Engineer officers:

Engineer Department
Washington, April 29, 1865

Sir:

In conformity with General Order No. 77, AGO, a copy of which is herewith enclosed, you will cause the same to be carried into effect without delay.

Your attention is to be given first, to suspending all unnecessary expenditures for services and material. No more work is to be done on any of the field fortifications by hired labor or purchased material.

You will then give your attention to the collection and preservation of all Engineer property, books, maps, plans, instruments and papers under your charge, and that of officers and others under your command, to the end that, the resources of the government shall be preserved and disposed of to insure the greatest economy with least possible expense.

In effecting this purpose you will request the Commanding General to furnish you with such store houses, means of transportation, service of troops, and store-keepers, as shall best secure the public interest.

As much of this property as may be needed for the use of the Army and Engineer service generally will be carefully preserved; the residue will be sold or otherwise disposed of, as shall hereafter be directed— the present purpose being to collect and preserve the property.

Richard Delafield,
General and Chief Engineer[5]

The War Department followed with another order in concert with the Engineer bureau's recommendations:

GENERAL ORDERS No. 87.

WAR DEPT., ADJT. GENERAL'S OFFICE,
Washington, May 9, 1865.

Concerning engineer property and labor on fieldworks.

Army and department commanders will at once cause to be collected and stored, at convenient depots, all tools, siege material, bridge equipage, and other engineer property not absolutely needed for immediate service with troops, and have inventories of property so collected forwarded to the Chief Engineer of the Army, with recommendation for its disposal. The latter will give the necessary instructions.

All labor on construction and repairs of field-works should now be done by troops; hired labor will not, therefore, be so employed, unless specially authorized from these headquarters or the Engineer Department; and no further purchases of engineer material for field-works will be made without similar authority, except in cases of urgent necessity.

By order of the Secretary of War:

E. D. TOWNSEND,
Assistant Adjutant-General.[6]

The Chief Engineer of the Defenses of Washington, Lieutenant Colonel Barton S. Alexander, had given considerable thought to what the end of the war would mean for the fortifications in his charge . On May 1, he wrote Chief Engineer, Richard Delafield:

"I had anticipated to some extent at least, the orders of the Secretary of War, and instructions of the Department by suspending operations on all new works and as far as practicable on all the old works of secondary importance, and since that time have confined operations to the more important forts, standing on prominent points, and commanding the approaches to the city.

To be specific, so that there may be no misunderstanding, I will add that my instructions contemplated the keeping up of twenty forts, ten on each side of the [Potomac] River - viz:
North of the Potomac
Fort Carroll, Fort Stanton, Fort Baker, Fort Mahan, Fort Lincoln, Fort Totten, fort Slocum, Fort Steevens, Fort Reno and Fort Sumner.
South of the Potomac
Fort Lyon, fort Ellsworth, Fort Worth, Fort Ward, Fort Richardson, Fort McPherson, Fort Whipple, Fort Morton, Fort C.F. Smith and Fort Ethan Allen.

This list, as will be seen, does not include either Fort Foote or Battery Rodgers, the two water batteries for the defense of the [Potomac] River approach to the city which I took for granted would be maintained.

Such was my idea of what ought to be done before I received the circular of the Department and such is still my opinion."[7]

Later, in the same report, Alexander wrote, "In issuing the orders to which I have alluded I supposed that I had reduced the number of works to a minimum." He then queried, "The question presented for consideration is one of policy. Does the government wish any of the works now constituting the defenses of Washington to be maintained? If so, is it desirable that the number of these works should be reduced to a minimum? If these questions are answered in the affirmative then all necessary orders have already been given and I shall in future confine my operations to finishing the work already commenced at the forts above designated. Holding these [forts] we command most of the approaches to the city and have the skeleton of a line of defence which can be readily put up again on the breaking out of a future war."[8]

Elaborating on his ideas, Alexander sent the following memorandum to the commander of the Defenses of Washington, Major General Christopher C. Augur:

List of forts and batteries arranged in classes in the order of their relative importance.

Designation of works north of the Potomac (first class): Forts Foote, Carroll, Stanton, Baker, Mahan, Lincoln, and Battery Jameson, Forts Totten, Slocum, Stevens, Reno, and Battery Reno, Fort Sumner.

South of the Potomac (first class): Battery Rodgers, Forts Lyon, Ellsworth, Worth, Ward, Richardson, McPherson, Whipple, Morton, (C. F. Smith, Ethan Allen.

It has been proposed to retain permanently the forts of the first class, as they occupy commanding positions, and If maintained will constitute the skeleton of a line of defense which may be easily built up again when circumstances require. It is difficult to say which of these forts is the-most important. They are arranged, therefore, in geographical position.

North of the Potomac (second class): Forts Greble, Meigs, fort on Kennedy s Hill, Forts Chaplin, Bunker Hill, De Russy, Kearny, Simmons and Mansfield (essentially one fort), Battery Cameron.

South of the Potomac (second class): Forts Willard, O'Rorke, Farnsworth, Weed, Barnard, Berry, Albany, Tillinghast, Strong, Marcy. The forts of this class are generally in good order, and would last many years without much expenditure of labor or money. They occupy positions which must be held when the city is threatened by a land attack. They are not so important, however, as the forts named in the first class.

North of the Potomac (third class): Forts Snyder, Ricketts, Wagner, Davis, Du Pont, circular fort, Fort Thayer, Battery Morris, Forts Saratoga, Slemmer, Batteries Smead, Russell, Forts Bayard, Gaines, Batteries Vermont, Martin Scott, Chain Bridge Battery, Batteries Kemble and Parrott.

South of the Potomac (third class): Fort Williams, Battery Garesche, Forts Reynolds, Scott, Runyon, Jackson, Craig, Cass, Woodbury, Corcoran, Bennett, Haggetty, two block-houses and battery in Hunting Creek Valley, one blockhouse on Leesburg turnpike, three block-houses on Aqueduct Bridge. This class embraces the works of least importance and should be first abandoned.

B. S. ALEXANDER,
Lieutenant-Colonel and Aide-de-Camp, Chief Engineer of Defenses.

Washington, DC, May 10, 1865.[9]

The Chief Engineer of the Army, Richard Delafield, had given some additional thought to the disposition of the Defenses of Washington and he wrote the Secretary of War, Edwin M. Stanton, on May 6, 1865, offering his views:

Engineer Department
Washington, D.C., May 6, 1865.

Hon. E. M. STANTON,
Secretary of War, Washington, D.C.:

SIR: The defenses of Washington at this time consist of seventy-four inclosed forts and armed batteries, each having a guard or garrison, and armed with 905 guns of various calibers, with magazine stores with powder and fixed ammunition amounting to about 200 rounds per gun, or 181,000 rounds. This system of defensive works envelopes the city, navy-yard, Alexandria, and Georgetown, and was constructed against rebel enemies who could approach by land from north, south, east, and west, and is about thirty-two miles in extent. The necessity for this extensive system of temporary works no longer exists, and I recommend that fifty-one of these forts and inclosed batteries be at once dismantled, the artillery and stores of all kinds withdrawn, and deposited either in the remaining twenty-three forts or at the arsenals, stores, and depots under charge of the different military departments of the army. After disarming, dismantling, and withdrawing the stores, a guard should remain to protect the property from fire and injury, and measures taken to restore the grounds to the rightful owners. To this end it is advisable, as far as practicable, to liquidate claims on the Government for the uses and changes made to the property by conveying to the owners the right and title to the buildings and fixtures, of timber on the bomb-proofs, magazines, and stockades of the several works; which if unacceptable to the claimants in full satisfaction for the use of the ground, changes, alterations, and removal of fences, woods, trees, and all others made by the authorities of the United States, the same shall be removed and materials in part sold in such manner as shall be found most advantageous to the public interest, and the residue stored as may be useful for the military service elsewhere. The works to be retained for the present will be:

On the north of the Potomac: Fort Carroll, Fort Stanton, Fort Baker, Fort Mahan, Fort Lincoln, Fort Totten, Fort Slocum, Fort Stevens, Fort Reno, and Fort Sumner; and on the south of the Potomac: Fort Lyon and three redoubts, Fort Ellsworth, Fort Worth, Fort Ward, Fort Richardson, Fort McPherson, Fort Whipple, Fort Morton, Fort C. F. Smith, and Fort Ethan Allen. The two river forts, to wit, Fort Foote and Battery Rodgers, will also be retained for the present. These twenty-three retained forts and redoubts occupy and command thirteen positions or lines of approach by roads or cover the cities of Alexandria, Georgetown, and Washington; its navy-yard and arsenal, and the roads from the north, west, south, and east, At a later period, after the fifty-one works and all their connecting lines of intrenchments have been vacated and ground restored to the owners, some of the remaining twenty-three may probably be dismantled and the grounds in like manner restored to their proprietors.

The preceding recommendation is founded upon the consideration that a large garrison is necessary for some time to come, and in part to be permanently stationed in and about this city for the protection of the national executive authorities, its archives, its costly and extensive public buildings, vieing with any of those in Europe for magnificence, elegance of architecture, durability, and fitness for the intended purposes; and its naval establishment and extensive ordnance depots, the value and cost of which is millions of dollars, and the destruction of which would be a serious loss and prejudice to the public welfare. Not less than 10,000 men at the present time, it is believed, will be necessary under all considerations to be retained in and about the city, and the twenty-three retained forts are selected with the view of best protecting the public interests and providing quarters and other accommodations for such a garrison . . .

Respectfully, your obedient servant,

RICH'D DELAFIELD,
Brigadier-General and Chief of Engineers[10].

Stanton read the report and referred it to the Commanding General of the Army, Major General U.S. Grant. On May 10, Grant wrote, "The recommendations of the chief engineer as to works in the defensive line around Washington and Alexandria to be dismantled and the manner of doing it are approved . . ."[11] The War Department then implemented the recommendations in the Special Orders No. 315, June 19, 1865, in the following section:

> 59. First. Upon the recommendation of the chief engineer, dated May 6, 1865, approved by the lieutenant-general, the major-general commanding the Department of Washington will at once give orders for the dismantling of the field-works, &c., constructed for the defense of Washington, with the following exceptions: North of the Potomac—Fort Carroll, Fort Stanton, Fort Baker, Fort Mahan, Fort Lincoln, Fort Totten, Fort Slocum, Fort Stevens, Fort Reno, and Fort Sumner; south of the Potomac—Fort Lyon and three redoubts, Fort Ellsworth, Fort Worth, Fort Ward, Fort Richardson, Fort McPherson, Fort Whipple, Fort Morton, Fort C. F. Smith, and Fort Ethan Allen; also the two river forts, Fort Foote and Battery Rodgers.
>
> Second. He will see that the forts above named are properly armed, making such changes in their present armaments as may be required by the interests of the service.
>
> Third. He will also see that the stores not required for those forts are properly stored and cared for, using temporarily such of the dismantled forts as may be required for those stores which cannot be properly cared for by the staff departments.
>
> Fourth. Until Fort McPherson is so far completed as to be ready for its armament and garrison Forts Tillinghast and Craig, immediately in front of this position, will be maintained.
>
> Fifth. The ground occupied by the defenses to be abandoned will be restored to their proprietors of loyal character, endeavors being first made to liquidate all claims for occupation and damage of every kind by transferring to them all the right and title to the buildings and fixtures of timber on the bombproofs, magazines, and stockades erected thereon. In the event that such arrangement is not made to liquidate the claims in full the buildings will be torn down and material transported to and used for construction of permanent defenses elsewhere, or sold, as may be found most advantageous. A sufficient guard will be, meantime, kept to protect the property from fire and injury.[12]

Reacting to this order, the U.S. Army's Department of Washington released its own issuance:

GENERAL ORDERS No. 89

HDQRS. DEPT. OF WASHINGTON,
TWENTY-SECOND ARMY CORPS,
June 23, 1865.

I. Under instructions contained in Special Orders, No. 315, current series, War Department, Adjutant-General's Office, of June 19, 1865, the following field-works are announced as composing the defenses of Washington: North of Potomac—Fort Carroll, Fort Stanton, Fort Baker, Fort Mahan, Fort Lincoln, Fort Totten, Fort Slocum, Fort Stevens, Fort Reno, Fort Sumner, and Fort Foote; south of Potomac—Fort Lyon and Redoubts Weed, Farnsworth, and O'Rorke, Fort Ellsworth, Fort Worth, Fort Ward, Fort Richardson, Fort McPherson, Fort Whipple, Fort Morton, Fort C. F. Smith, Fort Ethan Allen, and Battery Rodgers. All other forts, batteries, and blockhouses of the defenses of Washington will be at once dismantled, excepting Fort Tillinghast and Fort Craig, which will be maintained until Fort McPherson, immediately in the rear of the positions occupied by them, is so far completed as to receive its armament.

II. Under instructions to be issued through the chief of artillery of the department, and chief engineer of the defenses, division commanders will dispose of all ordnance and ordnance stores belonging to the forts to be dismantled, and make the necessary changes in the armament of the works to be retained.

II. Fort Greble (north of the Potomac) and Fort Corcoran (south of Potomac) will be used temporarily for the storage of such ordnance and ordnance stores as the chief of ordnance may designate.

IV. As soon as the artillery, ammunition, and other stores are removed from any fort, battery, or block-house, the garrison thereof will be withdrawn, and only sufficient guard left to protect the property. This guard will remain until further orders from these headquarters.

V. Such property and material belonging to the Engineer Department within the forts to be dismantled, as in the opinion of the chief engineer of the defenses may be needed for the completion of the forts to be retained, or is of such nature as would render it liable to injury, or to be stolen, will be at once removed to the works where needed, or turned into the nearest engineer depot.

VI. The chief of artillery and chief engineer of the defenses will render, with as little delay as practicable, to these headquarters reports of their action taken under the provisions of this order, and schedule exhibiting proper strength of garrison for each work to be retained.

VII. The chief quartermaster, Department of Washington, will furnish the necessary transportation for execution of this order.

By command of Major-General Parke:

J. H. TAYLOR,
Chief of Staff and Assistant Adjutant-General.[13]

So, in May and June, most of those Army officers who were involved in the ultimate disposition of the Defenses of Washington concurred, but did not necessarily agree on the way in which to achieve their goal. On May 20, Alexander admonished the Chief Engineer that, "In making arrangements for carrying into effect the instructions of the Department . . . in respect to the defence of the city, I find that if I am not allowed to incur expenditures for materials or for pay of hired men, I shall be forced to cease operations entirely in a few days from this time."[14] Then, on May 22, Alexander asked "to be supplied with twenty thousand dollars . . . to be applied to the Intrenchments for the defence of Washington for the current month. This amount will be mainly for the payment of wages of workmen . . ."[15]

Delafield replied on May 26, informing Alexander "that unless other instructions are received from the War Department no changes can be made in the orders . . . in reference to the defensive works of this city, . . ."[16] Although Alexander, and possibly others, thought that the Defenses of Washington held a special status and required more than the other defenses around the country, the War Department had decided specifically what was necessary. The orders issued to Alexander were final.

Alexander reported that during his May 1865 operations, "The force of hired workmen, mechanics and laborers was greatly reduced during the last month." He stated that this force had averaged 163 hired men and 15 enlisted men for the defenses north of the Potomac and 190 hired men and 446 enlisted men for the defenses south of the Potomac. In June, the force averaged 18 hired men and 135 enlisted men for the defenses north of the Potomac and 20 hired men and 230 enlisted men for the defenses south of the Potomac. By September 1865, the force averaged one enlisted man and 9 hired men for the defenses north of the Potomac and 15 enlisted men and 12 hired men for the defenses south of the Potomac.[17]

During this time, the work force performed a variety of renovation tasks. Alexander, in June 1865, reported to the Chief Engineer that during May his workforce had accomplished the following work on the "retained forts": sloping and sodding parapets, banquette slopes and traverses at Fort Foote; putting a stockade in front of the magazine at Fort Stanton; revetting the passageway at Fort Meigs; removing the old counterscarp gallery and erecting a new one at Fort Lincoln; reinforcing the parapet at Fort Ethan Allen; roofing, flooring, shelving and ventilating the new magazines at Fort McPherson; and repairing the lunette at Fort Strong. In June, the workforce built a counterscarp gallery and covered it with earth at Fort Lincoln; constructed an entrance and gateway, built a parapet and gravelled the terreplein at Fort Ward; laid gun platforms, constructed embrasures, built a new stone magazine and removed the old magazine, and put up a pole revetment at Fort Worth; laid gun platforms, made embrasures, and raised the right front bastion's parapet at Fort Ellsworth; built a traverse at the right end of the bombproof at Fort Lyon; and constructed two filling rooms and covered them with earth at Battery Rodgers. Engineer work on the "retained forts" in July included: sodding the parapet slopes at forts Carroll, Stanton, Baker, Mahan, Totten, Slocum, Stevens, Sumner, Whipple and Battery Reno; repairing the bridge at Fort Greble; putting a balustrade in the bomb-proof at Fort Ethan Allen; laying gun platforms at forts Lyon, Ellsworth, Ethan Allen and C.F. Smith; making embrasures at C. F. Smith; constructing stone magazines at forts Ethan Allen and Worth; and making and sodding banquettes at the gateway at Fort Ward. In August, the work included laying two gun platforms at Fort Reno; laying gun platforms at various "retained forts" South of the Potomac; sodding the parapet slopes at Fort Sumner; and constructing traverses and implement rooms at Battery Rodgers. Alexander reported no further work on the "retained forts" following the August work because the Engineers were not "to incur expenditures for hired labor" and "the Major General commanding the Department declined to furnish any large details of enlisted men."[18]

At those fortifications deemed expendable, the workforce removed pintle crosses, magazine lining, brass locks, hinges, and sandbags; dismantled buildings, dismounted artillery, and collected tools and other engineer property and hauled them to one of the four engineer camps. As time elapsed, the Army chose to maintain fewer and fewer of the forts necessitating the collection of even more engineer property.[19]

Given the great number and size of the fortifications in the Defenses of Washington, the work took some time to complete But, on January 13, 1866, Alexander reported, ". . . I closed up my office here, as far as it is possible to close it, before leaving; that I have discharged every person connected with the defenses except . . . Wm. H. Dickman . . . all money in my hands appertaining to the defences has been deposited to the credit of the Treasurer of the United States, except the sum of $159.52/100 which has been retained to pay bills yet outstanding."[20] Then on July 14, 1866, from Boston, MA, he wrote, "I have this day closed my accounts for defences of Washington by depositing in the Treasury to credit of the Treasurer of the

United States, the unexpended balance of funds received by me amounting to $582.67 the original certificate of which is respectively enclosed herewith."[21]   With the Civil War over, the country had quickly abandoned the elaborate fortification system around its capital.

Disposition of the Fortifications

What happened to the fortifications after the war. The Army had owned the land on which some of the fortifications were built, such as at Battery Vermont, and purchased, in January 1864, the land encompassing Fort Whipple. But, private individuals owned most of the subject land. Delafield, therefore, in his May 6, 1865 report, wrote that measures should be "taken to restore the grounds to the rightful owners."[22]

Restoring the land was only part of the problem. Besides losing control of their land during the war, the owners had suffered additional financial loss because they were unable to cultivate their fields. Many had lost even more because the Army destroyed fence rails, trees, and other property for a variety of purposes from fueling a warm fire; to furnishing materials for constructing gabions, fascines and fraise used in the fortifications; to providing a field of fire for the artillery.[23]

Colonel John G. Barnard, Alexander's predecessor as Chief Engineer of the Defenses of Washington, aptly described the Army's use of the land on which it built the fortifications:

> 'The sites of the several works being determined upon, possession was at once taken, with little or no reference to the rights of the owners or the occupants of the lands—the stern law of "military necessity" and the magnitude of the public interests involved in the security of the nation's capital being paramount to every other consideration. In one case a church, and in several instances dwellings and other buildings were demolished, that the sites might be occupied by forts. Long lines of rifle-trenches and military roads were located and constructed where the principles of defense or the convenience of communication required them, without regard to the cultivated fields or orchards through which they might pass. In addition to the ground immediately occupied by the defensive works, the lands in front for a distance of two miles were cleared of standing timber. At this work alone there were employed in the autumn of 1862 details of troops numbering from 2,000 to 3,000 men for a period of several weeks. The timber so cut down was used, so far as it was found to be suitable, in the construction of the forts, or for abatis.
>
> The injuries thus inflicted upon the citizens living along the lines, in the destruction and use of private property, were in the aggregate very considerable, and there were probably individual cases of extreme hardship; but, however much these evils might be deplored, they could not be avoided. No compensation for such damages or occupation of lands was made or promised, nor was it even practicable to make an estimate of their pecuniary amount. In some instances a statement of the number of acres denuded of timber, and a general description of its kind and quality, and in others of the number and kind of trees cutdown, was given to the owners, upon request being made therefor, as a supposed basis of future indemnity by the Government; but no general system of estimating damages was attempted."[24]

Some of the owners had already proffered claims for land occupation, use and damages. On December 15, 1862, B.T. Swart wrote that the Army had occupied his farm for Fort DeRussy, preventing him from cultivating his land to support his family, and felled his timber for buildings; he asked for rent and either permission to use his wood or receive recompense for it. Mrs. Mary Walker and L.E. Chittenden submitted claims for damages and rent of land occuppied by Fort Slocum, Fort Reynolds, and some camps, in 1864. In late 1863, Mrs. James C. Dwyer submitted a claim for the use of her 70 acre farm, near "Tennally Town", for Fort Reno; as a result, she received $50.00 per month rent for her land from the date of first occupation till the Army abandoned it in 1866." Mr. P.J. Buckey had received $50.00 per annum for rent of land on which Fort Bayard was erected and Samuel Shoemaker had received $50.00 per month rent for land on which Fort Mansfield was located.[25]

Realizing the possibility of numerous future claims, Delafield proposed, "To this end it is advisable, as far as practicable, to liquidate claims on the Government for the uses and changes made to the property by conveying to the owners the right and title to the buildings and fixtures, of timber on the bomb-proofs, magazines, and stockades of the several works." He considered the wood and other materials valuable enough to placate the owners.[26] The following notice appeared in the August 26, 1865 issue of *The Army and Navy Journal*:

> "An opportunity has been afforded by the Government to owners of farms upon which forts have been erected, to receive the buildings and other property left in dismantling the works as compensation for the occupation of the land. A few have already accepted the offer, but as there still remains a large amount of nvaluable property unaccepted, requiring guards for its protection, it is probable that the Government will shortly withdraw the offer, remove the buildings, &c., and leave the owners of lands the unpromising alternative of getting their claims for compensation through Congress."[27]

In spite of the value of wood and other materials at the forts, some owners, including Ellen J. King (Battery Parrott), Selby B. Scaggs (Fort Chaplin), Margaret B. Dangerfield (Battery Garesche) and Gilbert Vanderwerken (Fort Marcy), among others, refused to take the buildings and fixtures as full compensation for their use and damages claims. In these instances, Delafield admonished that " . . . if unacceptable to the claimants in full satisfaction for the use of the ground, changes, alterations, and removal of fences, woods, trees, and all others made by the authorities of the United States, the same shall be removed and materials in part sold in such manner as shall be found most advantageous to the public interest, and the residue stored as may be useful for the military service elsewhere."[28]

Responding to Delafield's decision or for some other reason, many owners changed their minds. By December 16, 1865, the Government had returned forts Marcy, Chaplin, Saratoga, Baker, Worth and Williams and batteries Cameron, Kemble, Garesche and Parrott to their owners with accompanying buildings and fixtures as compensation for occupation, use and damages. Each owner, in accepting the buildings and other property left in dismantling the works as just compensation for the occupation of the land, signed a statement similar to the following:

"This Witnesses

That Whereas the United States Occupied for Military Purposes a certain piece of land in the District of Columbia and erected thereon Battery Parrott, together with sundry buildings, and whereas upon determination this day of such occupancy the aforesaid buildings and improvements were by the United States granted to the owner of the land.

Now therefore I Ellen J. King, owner in fee simple of the land so occupied, for and in consideration of the sum of one dollar, the receipt of which is hereby acknowledged as well as in consideration of the buildings and improvements granted me as aforesaid, and by me accepted in full satisfaction for the use of said lands, do hereby release and quit claim forever all right, title, interest, and claim against the United States, to any damages that have accured or may hereafter accure to me by reason of the aforesaid military occupation of said land.

In witness thereof I have herewith set my hand and seal at Washington, D.C., this 28th day of October 1865.

(Signed) X [Ellen J. King]"[29]

Actually, some of the owners, including Ellen J. King, did not pay much attention to what they had signed. In May 1874, King submitted a claim for rent of her land for Battery Parrott, and for rails, posts and timber removed by the troops. In 1875 and 1876, she received compensation from the Treasury Department for rent and removal of timber.[30]

In certain instances, the Army felt that the accompanying buildings and fixtures were worth too much to turn over to the land owner and offered them money instead. To liquidate these valuable buildings and fixtures, the Army held auctions. In Alexander's accounts of auction sales during the week of December 9, 1865, he reported that he had received $1490 for the sale of abatis at five forts, a flagstaff, an implement house, the stockade in the rear of one fort, and timber, lumber &c. at three forts and "All other materials in Fort C.F. Smith." Specific winning bids were $65.00 for abatis at Fort Strong, $43.00 for the stockade in the rear of Fort C.F. Smith, and $605.00 for the timber, lumber, &c. inside of Fort Ethan Allen.[31]

Retained Fortifications

The Army retained some of the fortifications for military purposes. Fort Foote, MD, on the Potomac River, near Fort Washington, MD, served as a coastal fortification until 1878. The Army maintained Battery Rodgers, at Alexandria, VA, as a water battery on the Potomac river for a few years but budget cuts caused its abandonment. Fort Whipple, with its fortifications abandoned, became the home of a Signal School of Instruction for Army and Navy officers, established in 1869, and changed its name to Fort Myer in 1881. The Signal Corps also retained Forts Greble and Carroll, in Washington, DC, for a few years but soon abandoned them. Of all the forts, Fort Foote is the only one of the 68 forts in the Civil War Defenses of Washington system, which many considered the strongest defenses in the world when in use, that the Army maintained as a fortification for any period of time.[32]

Disposition of Related Property

The Army had constructed numerous roads during the Civil War to supply the fortifications in the Defenses of Washington, D.C. and to facilitate the movement of troops around, to, and from them; generally those military roads that aided the movement of traffic continued in use, as civilian roadways, including Military Road in Northwest Washington and in Arlington, VA, which today generally follow the routes of their original Civil War predecessors.[33]   After Early's Raid on Washington, the Quartermaster General, Montgomery C. Meigs, took possession of 1.033 acres, for the Government, as the future Battle Ground National Cemetery, and Congress acquired title to the land in February 1867.[34] Other sites, mostly associated with Early's Raid, existed in private ownership for several years after the war.[35] Examples include the seventeen Confederate dead of Early's Raid buried beneath a Confederate monument at Grace Church, in Silver Spring, MD, and nearby, the Francis Preston Blair's mansion. These related sites and others are discussed in subsequent chapters.

Endnotes

[1] Benjamin Franklin Cooling, *Mr. Lincoln's Forts: A Guide to the Civil War Defenses of Washington* (Shippensburg, PA: White Mane Publishing Company, 1988), 14-15.

[2] Longyear, John Munro. "Georgetown during the Civil War." *Georgetown Today*, 7, March 1975, 10.

[3] U.S., War Department, *The War of the Rebellion: A Compilation of the Official Records of the Union and Confederate Armies* (Washington, DC: The Government Printing Office, 1880-1901) (Hereafter referred to as AOR), (Serial 125) Series III, Volume IV, 1280-81.

[4] *AOR*, (Serial 97) Series I, Volume XLVI, Part 3, 875-76.

[5] *Engineer Orders and Circulars, Orders, Issuances*, 1811-1941, Records of the Office of the Chief of Engineers, Record Group 77, Archives I, National Archives and Records Administration (hereafter referred to as RG77).

[6] *AOR*, (Serial 97) Series I, Volume XLVI, Part 3, 1119.

[7] A2175, B.S. Alexander to Richard Delafield, May 1, 1865, Letters Received, 1826-66, RG77.

[8] A2175, B.S. Alexander to Richard Delafield, May 1, 1865, Letters Received, 1826-66, RG77.

[9] *AOR*, (Serial 97) Series I, Volume XLVI, Part 3, 1130.

[10] SW4529, Richard Delafield to E.M. Stanton, May 6, 1865, Letters Received, 1826-66, RG77; AOR, (Serial 97) Series I, Volume XLVI, Part 3, 1099-1100.

[11] Endorsements, SW4529, Richard Delafield to E.M. Stanton, May 6, 1865, Letters Received, 1826-66, RG77; *AOR*, (Serial 97) Series I, Volume XLVI, Part 3, 1101.

[12] *AOR*, (Serial 97) Series I, Volume XLVI, Part 3, 1285-86.

[13] *AOR*, (Serial 97) Series I, Volume XLVI, Part 3, 1293-94.

[14] A2180, B.S. Alexander to Richard Delafield, May 20, 1865, Letters Received, 1826-66, RG77.

[15] A2181, B.S. Alexander to Richard Delafield, May 22, 1865, Letters Received, 1826-66, RG77.

[16] A2184, B.S. Alexander to Richard Delafield, May 29, 1865, Letters Received, 1826-66, RG77.

[17] A2191, B.S. Alexander to Richard Delafield, June 6, 1865; A2232, B.S. Alexander to Richard Delafield, July 10, 1865; A2326, B.S. Alexander to Richard Delafield, October 17, 1865; Letters Received, 1826-66, RG77.

18 A2191, B.S. Alexander to Richard Delafield, June 6, 1865; A2232, B.S. Alexander to Richard Delafield, July 10, 1865; A2260, B.S. Alexander to Richard Delafield, August 2, 1865; A2299, B.S. Alexander to Richard Delafield, September 8, 1865; A2326, B.S. Alexander to Richard Delafield, October 17, 1865; A2331, B.S. Alexander to Richard Delafield, October 18, 1865; A2379, B.S. Alexander to Richard Delafield, December 5, 1865; Letters Received, 1826-66, RG77.

19 A2191, B.S. Alexander to Richard Delafield, June 6, 1865; A2232, B.S. Alexander to Richard Delafield, July 10, 1865; A2260, B.S. Alexander to Richard Delafield, August 2, 1865; A2299, B.S. Alexander to Richard Delafield, September 8, 1865; A2326, B.S. Alexander to Richard Delafield, October 17, 1865; A2331, B.S. Alexander to Richard Delafield, October 18, 1865; A2379, B.S. Alexander to Richard Delafield, December 5, 1865; Letters Received, 1826-66, RG77.

20 A2435, B.S. Alexander to Richard Delafield, January 13, 1866, Letters Received, 1826-66, RG77.

21 A2630, B.S. Alexander to Richard Delafield, July 14, 1866, Letters Received, 1826-66, RG77.

22 SW4529, Richard Delafield to E.M. Stanton, Letters Received, 1826-66, RG77; *AOR*, (Serial 97), Series I, Volume XLVI, Part 3, 1099; Fort Myer Post. The History of Fort Myer, Virginia. Special Centennial Edition of the *Fort Myer Post*. Fort Myer, VA: *Fort Myer Post*, [June] 1963, 4.

23 "Defenses of Washington, DC," Consolidated Correspondence File, 1794-1890, Special Files, 1794-1926; and #189, B.T. Swart, December 15, 1862, Claims and Related Papers for Damage to Property by Troops in the Service of the United States, 1861-65, Miscellaneous Claims, Claims Registers and Claims, 1839-1901, Central Records, Claims, 1839-1914; Records of the Office of the Quartermaster General, Record Group 92, Archives I, National Archives and Records Administration, Washington, D.C. (hereafter referred to as RG92); District of Columbia, Land Papers, 1794-1916, Lands, 1790-1916, Records Relating to Various Subjects; Land Releases, 1865, Defenses of Washington, 1861-66, Records of Detached Engineer Officers; and SW4579, L.H.T. to B.T. Swart, Letters Received, 1826-66; RG77.

24 John G. Barnard, *A Report on the Defenses of Washington, to the Chief of Engineers, U. S. Army, Corps of Engineers, Corps of Engineers Professional Paper No. 20* (Washington, DC: The Government Printing Office, 1871), 85.

25 De Russy, Fort (1865-66)," "Reno, Fort, DC, 1863, and "Defenses of Washington, DC," Entry 225, Consolidated Correspondence File, 1794-1890, Special Files, 1794-1926 and #189, S1138, B.T. Swart, December 15, 1862, Entry 843, Claims and Related Papers for Damage to Property by Troops in the Service of the United States, 1861-65, Miscellaneous Claims, Claims Registers and Claims, 1839-1901, Central Records, RG92; District of Columbia; Land Papers, 1794-1916, Lands, 1790-1916, Records Relating to Various Subjects and Land Releases, 1865, Defenses of Washington, 1861-66, Records of Detached Engineer Officers and SW4579, L.H.T. to B.T. Swart, Letters Received, 1826-66; RG77; Helm, *Tenleytown, D. C.*, 168.

26 SW4529, Richard Delafield to E.M. Stanton, Letters Received, 1826-66, RG77; *AOR*, (Serial 97) Series I, Volume XLVI, Part 3, 1099.

[27] *Army and Navy Journal, III,* August 26, 1865, 5.

[28] "Defenses of Washington, DC," Entry 225, Consolidated Correspondence File, 1794-1890, Special Files, 1794-1926," RG92; Entry 574, Land Releases, 1865, Defenses of Washington, 1861-66, Records of Detached Engineer Officers and SW4529, Richard Delafield to E.M. Stanton, Letters Received, 1826-66, RG77; Cooling, *Symbol, Sword and Shield* Second Revised Edition (Shippensburg, PA: White Mane Publishing Company, Inc., 1991), 238-39; *AOR*, (Serial 97) Series I, Volume XLVI, Part 3, 1099.

[29] "Defenses of Washington, DC," Entry 225, Consolidated Correspondence File, 1794-1890, Special Files, 1794-1926," RG92; Defences of Washington, List of transfers of Public property as compensation for damages and releases by the Claimants," December 16, 1865; and other papers, Land Releases, 1865, Defenses of Washington, 1861-66, Records of Detached Engineer Officers; RG77; Cooling, *Symbol, Sword and Shield* , 238-39.

[30] #1240, Book F, Box 86, and #3817, Book H, Box 125, Quartermaster Stores, Rent, Services, and Miscellaneous Claims, and #1417, Book 54, Box 15, Miscellaneous Claims, Document File, Claims Branch, 1861-1889, RG92.

[31] A2395, B.S. Alexander to Richard Delafield, December 12, 1865, Letters Received, 1826-66, RG77; Cooling, *Symbol, Sword and Shield* , 236; *The Army and Navy Journal, III,* November 25, 1865, 208.

[32] Leonard E. Brown, *Fort Stanton, Fort Foote and Battery Ricketts: Historic Structures Reports* (Washington, DC: Office of History and Historic Architecture, Eastern Services Center, National Park Service, 1970), 85-121; Cooling, *Mr. Lincoln's Forts,* 16, 47, 217-18, 225-32; Jacqui Handly, *Civil War Defenses of Washington, D.C.: A Cultural Landscape Inventory* (Washington, D.C.: The Government Printing Office [Falls Church Office, Denver Service Center, National Park Service], 1996), 45.

[33] Cooling, *Mr. Lincoln's Forts,* 15; C.B. Rose, Jr., "Civil War Forts in Arlington," *The Arlington Historical Magazine, 1* (October 1960), 25-26; Zack Spratt, "Rock Creek Bridges," Records of the Columbia Historical Society, 1953-56, Volumes 53-56, 107-08; O.E. Hunt, "Defending the National Capital," in Francis Trevelyan Miller, *The Photographic History of the Civil War* (10 Volumes, New York: The Review of Reviews Co., 1911), Volume 5, *Forts and Artillery,* 94.

[34] Cooling, *Mr. Lincoln's Forts,* 163-65; U.S., Army, Judge Advocate General, *United States Military Reservations, National Cemeteries, and Military Parks,* Edited by Lewis W. Call (Washington, D.C.: The Government Printing Office, 1910), 41.

[35] Cooling, *Mr. Lincoln's Forts,* 165; Benjamin Franklin Cooling, *Jubal Early's Raid on Washington in 1864* (Baltimore, MD: The Nautical and Aviation Publishing Company of America, 1989), 116, 238-39.

Chapter II

The "Fort-Capped Hills"

Post Civil War Washington

The Washington, D.C. area experienced many changes during the Civil War. Because it was the capital of the Union, much of the fighting occurred nearby, and the military stored a great deal of its munitions and equipment in and around the capital. Thousands of soldiers and sailors lived in the area. Freedmen, former slaves, flocked to the Union capital by the thousands. The war effort required a hefty increase in Government employment. From 1861 to 1865 the population of Washington, D.C. grew from 75,000 to 120,000.[1]

All of these people needed a place to live, causing a wartime real estate boom that continued for some time afterwards, as many residents in the post-war period speculated in land and property. The new landowners varied from the rich to the poor unskilled workman. A number of blacks were among the new landowners. During and immediately after the war, about 30,000 blacks migrated to the City, but few were able to own property. The U.S. Government had abolished slavery in Washington, DC in April 1862, compensating the former owners for over 3,000 slaves, none of whom owned property. Approximately 3,250 black men from the city served in the Union Army during the war, most of whom also had no property. Thus, by the end of the war, the majority of blacks living in Washington were without property or income. By 1867, though, blacks comprised about one-fifth of the city's property owners.[2]

Realizing that many problems pertaining to freedmen and other refugees would likely accelerate after the war, on March 3, 1865, Congress established the Bureau of Refugees, Freedmen, and Abandoned Lands, incorporating several former Government organizations. General Oliver Otis Howard served as chief of the Bureau. Administered by the Army, the Bureau attempted to oversee the rehabilitation of freedmen and other refugees by helping them obtain food, clothing, housing and education. It had a daunting task.[3]

In 1863, the Army had established a "Freedman's Village" on the Arlington estate, in Virginia, owned before the war by the Custis-Lee families. There the freedmen could live and farm. As the war progressed, more and more freedmen came to the village, and even more arrived after the war. Administered by the Army and by Treasury special agents during most of the war, the village came under the jurisdiction of the new Bureau of Refugees Freedmen and Abandoned Lands in 1865. Although conditions were not the best in the village, they were much better than what the freedmen faced, on their own, in the city. The Bureau provided them with rooms in barracks constructed to house soldiers and in former hospitals. It also established hospitals in the City to minister to the sick freedmen. Still, the Bureau was unable to help everyone, and many freedmen had to make their own way and find their own shelter.[4]

In some instances, these freedmen and other refugees lived in and around the recently vacated forts that were formerly in the Defenses of Washington. In many instances, the Army returned these forts to their former owners, who may or may not have had an immediate use for the land in spite of the real estate boom. Thus, some of the forts and their buildings sat unattended. They were prime targets for squatters, mostly poor freedmen who could find shelter and other items such as abatis, which made good firewood. Some observers commented on these squatters, but almost no one mentioned particular forts or individuals, making it difficult to document this habitation.[5] Following are some of these general accounts:

- "But around the slopes of the fort, among the bush and in the laurel clearing free negroes had built their cabins out of the wrecks of battery wagon and sentry-box, and down the paths that the cannoniers had made in the moist hill sides, negro men and women, with pails and bundles on their heads, went jogging steadily, as in the first listless experience of self-ownership."[6]

- "All the forts around or overlooking the city are dismantled, the guns taken out of them, the land resigned to its owners. Needy negro squatters, living around the forts, have built themselves shanties of the officers' quarters, pulled out the abatis for firewood, made cordwood or joists out of the log platforms for the guns, and sawed up the great flag-staffs into quilting poles or bedstead posts.
  "The strolls out to these old forts are seedily picturesque. Freedmen, who exist by selling old horse-shoes and iron spikes, live with their squatter families where, of old, the army sutler kept the canteen; but the grass is drawing its parallels nearer and nearer the magazines. Some old clothes, a good deal of dirt, and forgotten graves, make now the local features of war."[7]

- "The fifty-six forts (sic!) built in the early days of the conflict to defend the capital were still standing in the suburbs. Plundered of their lumber by nearby farmers, they now served as shelter for the many freedmen who had poured into the District from the nearby plantations of Maryland and Virginia; from the wrecks of battery wagons and sentry boxes, they had improvised the flimsiest constructions."[8]

A large number of freedmen settled in the area of Fort Reno in northwest Washington. Historian Judith Beck Helm noted: "Fort Reno was retained by the Army as late as January 1866, and many freed blacks continued to live there." In 1869, the heirs of the owner, Giles Dyer, sold the fort and surrounding area to Newall Onion and Alexander Butts, real estate developers. They subdivided the land into sections of a couple acres each, then divided the sections into building lots. This land was soon made available for rent or sale at reasonable prices. Some black squatters bought land. One descendent of an African American buyer said that his grandfather bought a lot for $25.9

The area, sometimes called "Reno City," contained about sixty houses in 1894. Around the turn of the century, the population of Tenleytown, where Reno City was located, included a population of 758 whites and 369 blacks. So even though some people have considered Reno City as a wholly black community, it was not. Helm wrote: "It would not be accurate to describe the Fort Reno area as a ghetto or even as an enclave." Also, although the National Park Service pamphlet "Fort Circle Parks: Civil War Defenses of Washington, Washington, D.C.," (1993) declares that "Fort Reno was designated a freedmen's village," the Federal government never officially designated or recognized Reno City as a freedmens' Village.[10]

Maintaining and Disposing of the Forts

Because the Army returned most of the forts in the Civil War Defenses of Washington to their owners, Government agencies were precluded from using them after the war. That is why it was difficult for the Government to reacquire many of the forts for public parks in the Twentieth Century. The owners cleared many of the fort features and built upon them, so nothing remains of a number of the original fortifications. The military used only a few of these fort sites during later wars— e.g., the Spanish-American War, World War I, and World War II.

Not all of the forts were immediately abandoned, making them inaccessible to squatters. It was not until March 1866 that the Army announced the closing of Forts Carroll, Stanton, Baker, Mahan, Lincoln, Totten, Slocum, Reno, and Sumner. Fort Strong, VA, on Arlington Heights, was not abandoned until March 20, 1869. The time-consuming removal of Government property at the forts and their temporary use for other purposes delayed their abandonment.[11]

In abandoning the forts, the Army had to consider the value of property at each site. Various branches of the Army — including engineer, quartermaster, ordnance, and signal — had property at the forts. Each branch was responsible for retrieving its property, but a great deal of the work devolved on the Engineer Department, which owned a large percentage of the property. The Army Engineers collected the property, returned what they needed to the depots, and sold what was of no use to them. The remainder was sold at auctions and general sales. The Engineers had to be mindful, however, of other Army branches' property at the forts and possible hazards, such as from ammunition, as they implemented their salvage operations.[12]

The Quartermaster Department also played a significant role in the dismantling and abandoning of the forts. Some of the property at the forts — encompassing a variety of items, from buildings, wagons, animals, and door hinges — were Quartermaster Department property, which it collected and returned to its depots. In some instances, the Quartermaster Department sold property at auctions or in general sales. In addition, the Army often ordered the Quartermaster Department to furnish transportation for the movement of troops and property. The Quartermaster Department also furnished horses, equipment, forage and other items to troops stationed at the forts.[13]

In August 1867, the commander of the Department of Washington wrote to the Chief of Ordnance, asking how much longer he needed Fort Greble as an ordnance depot. The Ordnance Department had received permission to store ordnance and ordnance stores at Fort Greble as well as at one or two of the Virginia forts. When it could do so, the Ordnance Department removed its property to the Washington Arsenal, now Fort McNair, or transferred it to a garrisoned fort. The hazards of moving ammunition and the difficulties of transporting heavy and siege artillery prevented the quick disposition of these items.[14]

The infant Army Signal Corps, which played a valuable part in the Civil War, had some continuing requirements in the post-war period. In 1866, the Army allowed the Chief Signal Officer of the Army, Brigadier General Albert J. Myer, to use Forts Greble and Carroll, and Battery Greble. Then, in 1868, Myer requested and received control over Fort Greble as a signal communications school for instruction, the first of its kind, in electric telegraphy and visual signaling, based on his manual. Field practice was an important aspect of the school. In January 1869, however, Myer moved the school from Fort Greble and soon established it at Fort Whipple, VA.[15]

Of course, the Army did not abandon all of the forts at once, so it had to make special arrangements for disposition of property at various times. Thus, when the Army finally decided to abandon Battery Rodgers, VA, it could not fully vacate the fortification until the Ordnance Department transferred the 15-inch gun mounted on centre pintle carriage to Fort Washington, MD, reportedly to save money. Likewise, various officers informed the Engineer Department that a great deal of engineer property was also at Battery Rodgers. In October 1866, an officer directed the Ordnance Sergeant at Fort Corcoran, VA, to compile a complete list of all property at that place by morning to assist in readily deciding on disposition. When Fort Ellsworth was dismantled, authorities transported all of the guns to the Washington Arsenal. Thus, the Army had to coordinate the transfer of military and civilian personnel, as well as the property of the various departments, before abandoning the fort.[16]

At times, the Army chose to withdraw troops from forts before all property was removed. It, therefore often assigned an Ordnance Sergeant to the fort to guard all Army property until removed and to look after the installation. The Army had resorted to this practice for sometime, especially at the seacoast fortifications, many of which had no garrsions before the war. Stationing an Ordnance Sergeant at a fort sometimes created its own peculiar problems. In one instance, to prevent starvation of dependents, the Army had to officially designate the wife of the Ordnance Sergeant at Fort Greble a laundress so that she could receive rations. In a few instances, the Army hired civilian caretakers to look after military installations.[17]

The Army used some of the forts as prisons. Even before the war was over, Division headquarters ordered the bombproofs cleared at the forts in the Defenses of Washington to house prisoners; as a result, Fort Strong, VA, received 150 prisoners. *The Army and Navy Journal* of March 10, 1866, reported that Fort Whipple, VA, would be a prison for all "colored" prisoners sentenced by the military to more than 60 days incarceration. A later article in the same periodical, mentioned that the prisoners from the Old Capitol Prison in Washington, D.C., had also been transferred to Fort Whipple.[18]

Relationships between the garrisons at the forts and the citizens in the neighborhood was strained at times. The officers and men, like any other armies throughout history, did things that irritated the nearby residents. In some instances, the problem escalated from irritation to confrontation. In August 1865, Mr. Thomas Murphy, who lived near Fort Totten, complained of "depredations" upon his crops by troops at the fort. Edward N. Lucas, on March 7, 1866, complained that "he was assaulted and badly beaten by colored soldiers from Fort Corcoran at the Aqueduct Bridge yesterday." Any such accusation required a thorough investigation and, possibly, a court martial or trial. The Army wished to maintain a good relationship with the local citizens, and therefore usually went to great extremes to accommodate them.[19]

Maintaining Maritime Defenses

Although the Army abandoned the capital's land defenses after the Civil War, it continued to defend the maritime approaches to the city in expectation of foreign incursions or invasions. The Board of Engineers for Fortifications spent some time studying the defensive requirements to prevent such waterborne attacks. In the immediate post-war period, it contemplated the use of Forts Washington and Foote, in Maryland, and Battery Rodgers, at Alexandria, VA, to defend the Potomac River approaches to the capital. Battery Rodgers, erected during the Civil War as part of the Defenses of Washington, was a water battery that some thought could continue to defend the Potomac River. In April 1870, William P. Craighill, Baltimore District Engineer chief, reported to the Chief of Engineers that the Board of Engineers for Fortifications was considering Battery Rodgers as a seacoast defense installation and that he would soon visit the site and conduct an examination; Craighill, therefore, requested that the Chief of Engineers' office send him some maps and plans of the battery. On May 4, Craighill reported that he had visited the battery and the Board was considering it for emplacement of large guns "should an interior line of defense thereabout become necessary." On June 9th, Craighill informed the Chief of Engineers that the Board had decided against "further occupation" of Battery Rodgers. The Board still needed fortifications on the Potomac River and decided to hold on to Forts Washington and Foote, with some changes.

Much later, the Army erected concrete gun batteries for guns mounted on disappearing carriages at Fort Washington and the new Fort Hunt, directly across the river. As the caliber and range of coast defense guns increased, preventing enemy ships from entering Chesapeake Bay, the defenses on the Potomac River became obsolete. Forts Washington and Hunt were later used for non-coast defense purposes through World War II.[20]

Of all the fortifications in the Civil War Defenses of Washington, Fort Foote was the only one that continued to serve as a fortification. The fort was deemed important because this "work forms the inner line of defense of the channel of approach by water to Alexandria and the cities of Washington and Georgetown." On October 15, 1865, Acting Assistant Inspector General, J.B. Campbell, wrote that he had visited Fort Foote "since the late heavy rains, and find that considerable damage, has resulted to the work from them. . . bomb-proofs leak, slides of earth, recommend that the debris be removed." The Board of Engineers for Fortifications had studied the coast defense needs of the capital and the Potomac River and decided to retain Fort Foote, suggesting the "modification of this work and erection of an additional battery of the heaviest guns" north of the fort on Rozier's Bluff. After securing a title to the land on which Fort Foote was located in 1872-73, Congress appropriated $25,000 for it in the fiscal year ending June 30, 1874. The Engineers accomplished some of the necessary work then but due to the lack of further appropriations, they never completed it. When possible, the Fort Foote garrison undertook some cleanup, maintenance and construction.[21]

Various companies from the Second, Third, Fourth and Fifth U.S. Artillery Regiments, Maine Coast Guard, Fourteenth Pennsylvania Reserves Light Artillery, and 14th New York Artillery garrisoned the fort until the Army ordered Company I, Second U.S. Artillery Regiment, withdrawl from Fort Foote on November 10, 1878. From that point on, an Ordnance Sergeant or caretaker looked after the fort. In 1885, one officer reported: "At the present time the condition of the work [Fort Foote] may be described as one of utter dilapidation." Another officer wrote, "In their present conditions these two works [Forts Foote and Washington] would give but a feeble protection to the capital of the nation and its naval establishment." The Army held title to Fort Foote until after World War I. Some authors reported that the Corps of Engineers used Fort Foote as a training ground for recruits at times between 1902 and 1918. Unfortunately, official records have not been found to document this use.[22]

When designing Fort Foote and Battery Rodgers, the Army Engineers also urged the building of obstructions that could be moored in the Potomac River, near Fort Foote, to help impede the movement of enemy ships. In 1863, Brevet Major General John G. Barnard, the principle designer of the Civil War Defenses of Washington, requested $300,000. to build these obstructions. On July 2, 1864, Congress appropriated $300,000. for "obstructions to be moored in the Potomac River to render the shore batteries more efficient for the protection of Washington against maritime attack." Barton S. Alexander designed the obstructions, which some termed the "Alexandrine Chain," described as "a series of floats holding up a 400-foot-long chain with 23 anchors . . .." Unused during the war, the Army stored the obstructions in a shed at Fort Foote, "in charge of a watchman." In September 1868, the Chief of Engineers suggested to the Secretary of War that the Navy might test the obstructions. But when the Secretary of War brought up the subject in a cabinet meeting, the Secretary of the Navy declared the obstructions worthless and a waste, influencing all present to drop the proposal. Thus, no one ever tested or used the obstructions, and they slowly decayed in their shed at Fort Foote. [23]

Of the various fortifications in the Civil War Defenses of Washington, Fort Whipple, on Arlington Heights, VA, is the only one that the Army has occupied continuously to the present day. The suggested abandonment of Fort Whipple at various times in the immediate post-war period, never occurred. Fourth U.S. Artillery Regiment detachments were at Fort Whipple, from 1865 to 1867, and Company I, Twelfth U.S. Infantry Regiment, was there in 1868. By March 1866, Fort Whipple was a military prison, for those prisoners from the Old Capitol prison and "a place of confinement for all colored prisoners sentenced by military authority for a longer period than sixty days." In March of 1869, the Chief Signal Officer of the Army, Brigadier General Albert J. Myer, occupied the fort as the new location of the Signal School for Instruction of Army and Navy officers. By 1872, new construction, mostly for the Signal School, had removed most of the vestiges of the Civil War period fortifications. The school remained at Fort Whipple until 1886. Myer died in 1880 and the Army renamed the fort in his honor in February 1881. Fort Myer became a cavalry post in 1887. In the period before World War I, important airplane flight demonstrations occurred at Fort Whipple, 1908-09.[24]

Post War Changes in the Military

Numerous post-war organizational changes in the military affected the Washington, D.C. area and the Defenses of Washington. During the Civil War, the United States Armed Forces greatly expanded in a number of ways to prosecute the war. Then, in the post-war period, it had to cut back. The Army abandoned hundreds of forts, posts, camps, and stations throughout the country. They sent most of the volunteer units home and reduced the number of Regular Army troops.

These reductions required organizational changes, especially in the Washington, D.C. area. In April 1865, the Department of Washington changed the boundaries and names of the districts within it: the District of Alexandria comprised all troops south of the Potomac River, except the Northern Neck, south of the railroad from Fredericksburg and Aquia Creek Landing, with headquarters at Alexandria. The District of Washington embraced the area north of the Potomac River, except the City of Washington and the area between the Potomac and the Patuxent rivers, south of the Piscataway, with headquarters in Washington, D.C.

In June 1865, the War Department announced that the Department of Washington would encompass the District of Columbia, the counties of Anne Arundel, Prince George's, Calvert, Charles, and Saint Mary's, in Maryland, and Fairfax County, in Virginia, with its headquarters at Washington. The Department of Virginia, with headquarters at Richmond, embraced the entire State of Virginia, except Fairfax County and the line of the Baltimore and Ohio Railroad. The Department of Washington then discontinued the districts of Alexandria and Washington in the Summer of 1865.

With all these changes, the Department of Washington, on August 5, 1865, placed Brigadier General J.A. Haskins, whose headquarters was in Washington, in command of all troops serving in the forts North and South of the Potomac River. Also, due to the "dismantling of the forts and reduction of troops in the Department of Washington, "the "Defences of Washington" were discontinued on April 30, 1866. From then on, Forts Foote and Whipple, and Battery Rogers would report directly to the department.[25]

Memorializing the Defenses

While the Army was busy dismantling and abandoning the Civil War Defenses of Washington, one man was memorializing them. Brevet Major General John G. Barnard, who designed and oversaw much of their construction, remained with the Corps of Engineers after the war. Although he was occupied with other duties as a member of the Board of Engineers for Fortifications, located in New York, General Barnard found the time to complete his report. In the immediate post-war years, he compiled what became *A Report on the Defenses of Washington, to the Chief of Engineers, U. S. Army, Corps of Engineers, Corps of Engineers Professional Paper No. 20*, published by the Government Printing Office in 1871.[26]

Barnard worked on this report for sometime before its completion and wrote the Office of the Chief of Engineers in Washington, D.C., numerous times, requesting documents and drawings. In January 1869, the Chief of Engineers authorized him to hire someone to help in the preparation of his report and at other times he asked permission to temporarily hire others, including a "draughtsman". He asked the Engineer Department in April 1870 what was intended for his report, stating that the text was finished but the drawings were not. On June 8, 1870, he informed the Engineer Office that a Mr. Farrell would soon deliver, by hand, the text of the report and 30 sheets of drawings. A few weeks later, on June 27, Barnard reported that he had sent a box that day with 153 sheets of drawings, as well as other maps, photographs, letters, telegrams, and record books. Justifying his endeavors, Barnard wrote, "The Works originally commenced after the common type of 'field works,' ultimately became, owing to the necessity of greater permanence and more perfect arrangements for the use and preservation of the armaments and accommodation and protection of the garrison, types of a kind of construction scarcely known before, and of which it seemed to me some record should be preserved." When the Government published the report in 1871, it generally was received well. The one man who had led a raid on the Defenses of Washington, Jubal Early, wrote that it was a "valuable contribution . . . made to the history of an important episode" [meaning Jubal Early's Raid on Washington].[27]

The report was quite technical and provided good military engineering information for many, but at least one military scholar required more. Captain John Bigelow, 10th U.S. Cavalry, wrote the Chief of Engineers on March 5, 1896 asking for "the details of the construction of the timber revetment used in the defenses of Washington"as mentioned on page 64 in Barnard's report, specifically: 1. The fitting of the horizontal capping pieces and vertical pieces to each other; 2. The fitting of the anchor ties to the horizontal capping pieces and to the anchor logs; 3. The distance between anchor ties; and, 4. The length of an anchor log. Bigelow, as Professor of Military Science And Tactics at the Massachusetts Institute of Technology, needed the information for his class in military engineering. Along with an explanation, Bigelow received a "traced sketch showing the details of fitting the horizontal and vertical pieces together, and the anchor ties to the horizontal capping pieces and to the anchor logs." He replied that what he had received answered all of his questions except "the manner of attaching the tie piece to horizontal capping piece." Captain George W. Goethals, famous later for his work on the Panama Canal, replied that the "anchor tie should be attached by notching and spiking as shown in the inclosed sketch." Few others appeared to require such specific information.[28]

The Abandoned Forts - Describing What Remained

After the abandonment of the fortifications, few thought much of them except, possibly, when their remains were impediments to development. Little can be found in the newspapers, periodicals or City and Federal Government records about them in the period from about 1867 to the late 1890's. Some descriptions, however, are available in memoirs, guidebooks, and other writings relating to the Washington, D.C. area. In 1869, for example, John B. Ellis observed the following while riding in a train approaching Washington from the northeast, ."On either side of the road, we see, crowning these eminences, the grim red lines of the earthworks built for the defence of the Capital; each with its lonely, towering flag-staff from which once flapped in defiant pride the starry banner of the Republic, standing out against the blue sky like so many ghostly sentinels keeping solemn watch over the scenes they once guarded so well."[29]

Another 1869 account reports worse conditions, "About two miles outside of Washington, and completely encircling the city, is a chain of fortifications, completely connected by a military-road, forming a boulevard, which, by the aid of trees and shrubbery, judiciously cared for, would be equal to the famed drives surrounding the city of Paris. All of the fortifications on the north and east sides have long since been dismantled and are now either grass-grown or leveled with the surrounding earth, and completely obliterated by the farmer's ploughshare."[30]

George Alfred Townsend, a journalist, was one of the most widely read newspaper men from the Civil War to the end of the century. He worked for a variety of newspapers around the country, but lived, most of the time, in the Washington, D.C. area and wrote a great deal about what went on there. In 1873, he published a book, *Washington, Outside and Inside. A Picture and A Narrative of the Origin, Growth, Excellences, Abuses, Beauties, and Personages of Our Governing City,* that includes a number of interesting and poetic comments about the forts as they were in that year.

"I climbed the high hills one day on the other side, and pushing up by-paths through bramble and laurel, gained the ramparts of old Fort Stanton. How old already seem those fortresses, drawing their amphi-theatre around the Capital City! Here the scarf had fallen off in places; the *abatis* had been wrenched out for firewood; even the solid log platforms, where late the great guns stood on tiptoe, had yielded to the farmer's lever, and made, perhaps, joists for his barn, and piles for his bridge. The solid stone portals opening into bomb-proof and magazine, still remained strong and mortised, but down in the battery and dark subterranean quarters the smell was rank, the floor was full of mushrooms; a dog had littered in the innermost powder magazine, and showed her fangs as I held a lighted match before me advancing. Still the old names and numbers were painted upon the huge doorways beneath the inner parapet: "Officers quarters, 21," "Mess, 12," "Cartridge Box, 7."[31]

Following are a few other descriptions written at the time.

•   "What a picturesque and stirring crime is war! Suggestively useless are the monuments it leaves, but touching the imagination far more than the lordliest architecture of peace. Now do we feel among these shriveled moats and salients that the Capital city of our country has some surroundings to make it an inspiration. These wrecks of its defences will be some day the picnic haunts of curious patriotism, when Washington has grown to be a great city. Greater than its founders ever wished!"[32]

•   "To comprehend this city further, climb to the dome of the Capitol. It is enveloped by a range of fort-capped hills, half in Maryland, half in Virginia." [33]

•   "All the forts around or overlooking the city are dismantled, the guns taken out of them, the land resigned to its owners. . . . Still the huge parapets of the forts stand upright, and the paths left by the soldiers creep under the invisible gun muzzles. Old boots, blankets, and canteens rot and rust around the glacis; the woods, cut down to give the guns sight, are overgrown with shrubs and bushes. Nature is unrestingly making war upon War. The strolls out to these old forts are seedily picturesque. . . . Some old clothes, a good deal of dirt, and forgotten graves, make now the local features of war."[34]

- "Relics of the war are observed [from the steamboat Arrow], for many a mile, in broken wharves, erected at great expense, and now broken up for fuel; in the forests cut off to the stumps to give artillery space for play, and in pounds for horses; fields trampled bare by camps and always the high, naked hills upholding their airy ramparts two hundred feet above the water."[35]

- "We leave behind the grassy battery of Alexandria, where cows eat the moss from broken gun-carriages, the lighthouse spire, and the Cameron Cove, and, crossing to Maryland again, stop at Fort Foote, the only earthwork of the war still kept in order and garrisoned. It is a strong position, flanked by a bay and swamp, and steep as the heights of Abraham at Quebec. Four miles below, on the same side, is Fort Washington, a stone work, blown up in 1814, but now restored and bristling with guns, and as picturesque a spot as one can see."[36]

In 1873, Mary Clemmer Ames, who lived in the city, observed that, "Flowers blossom on the ramparts of the old forts, so alert with warlike life ten years ago. The army roads, so deeply grooved then, are grass-grown now. . . . Peace, prosperity and luxury have taken the place of war, of knightly days and of heroic men."[37] Randolph Keim, who published a number of editions of a guidebook on Washington, D.C, reported in the 1874 edition that, "The ruins of the now dismantled and deserted Defenses of Washington may yet be seen on almost every eminence in the vicinity of the city."[38]

In 1887, a "National Drill Encampment" occurred in Washington, D.C. *A Souvenir of the Federal Capital and of the National Drill and Encampment*, published for the event, included the following description, "These fortifications and batteries, with their green sod walls and yawning embrasures, from which the black muzzles of huge guns peered out menacingly upon every exposed height, were the most prominent and suggestive features of the landscape as one approached Washington from any direction during the latter years of the war. Today, of all these defenses, only a few mounds of earth remain."[39]

One Civil War cavalryman returned to Washington many years after the war, and, after visiting many of the old forts in Northern Virginia, left this account:

> In 1898 the writer was entertained for several days by Comrade Besley and his pleasant family, at Ashgrove, near Falls Church. The two rode around the wide semicircle of the outer fortifications, from Fort Buffalo on the north to Fort Lyon on the south. Some of the works had remained unchanged except by rain and frost. Some were covered with bushes and young trees. Camp Kearney was a goat pasture. The old headquarters house was going to ruin. The walls were standing, but the windows were gone and the doors were broken down. The basement where the officers' mess had feasted, was now the stable of the four-footed creatures of the pasture field.[40]

Perhaps, though, the most useful description of the forts formerly in the Defenses of Washington, is "The Present Condition of the Defenses of Washington, Built during the Civil War, 1861-1865," in Frank L. Averill's *Guide to the National Capital and Maps of Vicinity including the Fortifications*, published in 1892, because it provides detailed specific information on each of the forts. This account, therefore, is reproduced in its entirety as a status report on the fortifications at that particular time as Appendix A.

Early Efforts to Preserve the Forts

By the 1890s, some individuals and organizations began to advocate the preservation of, at least, some of the forts in the Defenses of Washington. Fort Stevens, which bore the brunt of Jubal Early's 1864 attack, suffered the same neglect as the other forts in the Civil War Defenses of Washington. One man, William Van Zandt Cox, whose father lost his life in the war, bought a great deal of the fort and in May 1899 offered to donate the fort, provided he could "erect half a dozen neat, two-story, six-room frame houses on the part that does not in any way encroach upon the fortifications . . ." In 1897, Cox, along with General Horatio G. Wright, commander of the Sixth Corps at the time of Jubal Early's Raid on Washington, in 1864, and another Union General, David S. Stanley, examined the deteriorated condition of Fort Stevens. Various individuals founded the Fort Stevens Lincoln Military Park Association to seek a park encompassing the former battlefield around Fort Stevens. The Associated Survivors of the Sixth Army Corps of Washington, D.C. also wrote in favor of a Fort Stevens battlefield park. The Brightwood Avenue Citizen's Association of the District of Columbia proposed that in addition to the Fort Stevens site, the United States should "purchase enough land to establish a battle-field park in connection with Forts DeRussy and Reno."[41]

Various patriotic organizations, both Union and Confederate, adopted resolutions favoring the establishment of an "Early's Raid on Washington" battlefield park. The Union Veterans Union, representing 100,000 veterans, voted to petition Congress to appropriate enough money "to purchase Fort Stevens and mark the only battlefield in the District of Columbia." Patriotic organizations such as the Grand Army of the Republic, the Loyal Legion of the United States, and the Women's Relief Corps, took part in ceremonies at Fort Stevens on Memorial Day, Flag Day, and on July 11, the day commemorating the battle. The Sixth Corps held a reunion in Washington in 1915 and had memorial and other activities at the fort. On November 7, 1911, about 4,500 attended a ceremony at Fort Stevens unveiling a rough stone marking the site where President Abraham Lincoln stood when viewing enemy troops during his visit to the fort during the battle.[42]

Congress considered numerous bills to establish a Fort Stevens—Lincoln National Military Park in the period between the turn of the century and the beginning of World War I, but to no avail. Perhaps the Secretary of War's 1902 comments had a great deal to do with the early fate of a Fort Stevens park as he wrote, "I think that if Congress considers it prudent to devote any more money for establishing battlefield parks, the places recommended in my Annual Report for 1899, which would include the battlefields of Fredericksburg, Salem Church, Chancellorsville, the Wilderness, and Spottsylvania Court House should be selected rather than Fort Stevens."[43]

Thus, a March 27, 1911 *Evening Star* article reported that "The ramparts of Fort Stevens have been leveled, with the exception of a section at the west end of the works. Washington's suburbs have grown around the fort and invade it. A small street crosses the parade ground of the fort and a row of small frame houses has been built there. Part of the north face of the fortification which fronted the southern forces remains, though the breastworks have been considerably worn down and the fronting ditch half filled by the wear of the seasons." A March 22, 1911 *Evening Star* headline stated, "Old Fort Stevens Sold, Purchased by Syndicate of Virginia and Maryland Capitalists," including "the old rifle pits and a large part of the Fort Stevens fortifications." Many thought that Fort Stevens could not be saved.[44]

In 1906, 34 residents and businesses of Northeast Washington championed a bill to make old Fort Thayer, near Langdon, a public park to preserve the fort. The Washington Park Commission also recommended it for a park, stipulating that it could be purchased for 10 cents per square foot and that it must be done immediately or it would be developed. The Commission noted that the northeast part of Washington had no park of any description and, therefore, submitted photographs of the fort demonstrating its good preservation status. The owners, Henry Vieth and Glenn E. Husted, wrote a letter stating that they were glad to sell the land with the fort on it to the City at a reasonable price if done soon, but if not they would need to grade it and sell it for building lots. Congress did not act, however, so the Commission resubmitted a bill in 1908, with a slight increase in price of 12 cents per square foot. The Committee on Public Buildings and Grounds returned an adverse report. A short time later, someone reported that Fort Thayer was completely gone.[45]

In January 1904, the Senate considered a bill to establish a national military park at Fort Reno. Referred to the Committee on Military Affairs, it provided that the fortifications there would be restored to their "original condition so far as practicable," although the construction of a reservoir and water tower on the site had removed the last vestiges of the fortifications, and that the commissioners would investigate and report to the Secretary of War the "condition of the other fortifications which surrounded Washington during the civil war, with their suggestions as to what action is necessary for their preservation." The Secretary of War effectively killed the bill by reiterating that the required expenses for the already authorized battlefields was too great already and that, "The National Government can not own and take care of all the spots of historic interest in the United States." Similar bills were introduced in the House of Representatives about the same time but they also failed.[46]

In 1912, the preservationists for the Civil War Defenses of Washington finally won a victory. In January 1912, the East Washington Heights Citizens' Association submitted a resolution to Congress "for purchase of Forts Davis and Dupont for park purposes." On June 24, a law went into effect that, among other things, provided for the condemnation of land to "preserve the sites of Fort Davis and Fort Dupont for park purposes, and to provide a connecting highway between" them. It also appropriated money to pay for the land. "These parks were to become a part of the District of Columbia public park system and would be under the control of the Chief of Engineers of the U.S. Army. The District Commissioners acquired 16.55 acres of what would become the Fort Dupont Park and transferred it to the Park Office in 1916. No further actions pertaining to this law occurred before or during World War I but, both forts did become parks later.[47]

In spite of some early preservation defeats, there seemed to be growing public interest in saving some of the Civil War Defenses of Washington. Also, a related project offered assistance in preserving some of the fortifications. In 1872, Francis P. Blair, who testified on "Affairs in the District of Columbia" before the House of Representatives Committee for the District of Columnia, on April 10, replied to the question, "You believe in the policy of getting uniform grades?":

> "I do; and carrying them through the city and into the District beyond Boundary Street. ... The next grade brings us to the circuit of forts that protected the city during the late war. The roads made to unite theses defenses by the soldiers formed an outer circle to Boundary Street, two miles beyond. They are located on eminences that command the country on both sides of the circuit, while the city is invisible and sheltered by the first elevation that surrounds it...
>
> But the improvement of greatest value, as most comprehensive, is that which proposes to finish the military road which unites the forts around the city. It is to become a grand avenue from the Soldiers' Home westward to the first bridge on the road between Fort Stevens and Fort De Russey, and thence carried along the stream of Rock Creek and the road on Broad Branch they blend into one main avenue, sloping with easy grade the 500 feet at the District line, along the current of Rock Creek to its junction with the Potomac, making the most romantic, picturesque drive to be found anywhere."[48]

Before the end of the century, City Engineer Commissioner William H. Powell championed the establishment of "a new drive-way through the suburbs of Washington to be called 'Fort Drive,' and include in its winding ways some of the most important of the fortifications which served as the Defenses of Washington during the rebellion . . ." An Act of March 2, 1893 provided that the City Commissioners establish a permanent highway plan and in the planning and discussion sessions, 1893-98, "serious consideration was given . . . to the construction of a Fort to Fort Drive." No surprise then, that the Fort Drive appeared on the 1898 District of Columbia highway map.[49]

1900 was the hundreth anniversary of the capital of the United States in Washington, D.C. The Senate, therefore, chose to authorize the Committee on the District of Columbia to prepare a proper celebration and "map out a comprehensive plan for the future development of Washington extending the L'Enfant Plan to cover the entire District of Columbia." The District Committee created a "Park Commission" that became known as the McMillan Commission. Composed of Daniel H. Burnham, Charles F. McKim, Augustus Saint Gaudens and Frederick Law Olmsted, Jr., the Commission submitted a park plan.[50]

The McMillan Commission's 1901 report, *The Improvement of the Park System of the District of Columbia*, discussed and recommended the Fort Drive; "While for the reasons already discussed no systematic series of minor reservations has been selected for the outlying districts, it is necessary to mention the chain of forts which occupied the higher summits in the northern part of the central section, extending from Fort Stevens, near Rock Creek Park, to Fort Thayer, near the Reform School." Further, to connect the "the series advantage is taken of the street laid out for the purpose in the highway plans, but it should be increased to a more liberal width than now provided, which is only 90 feet between houses, the same as H Street in the city." East of the Anacostia, "a similar chain of hilltop forts marks the point of most commanding view" and they "can be linked together readily by means of the permanent system of highways." But, nothing of any consequence pertaining to the "Fort Drive" occurred until after World War I.[51]

Endnotes

[1] James H. Whyte, *The Uncivil War: Washington during the Reconstruction 1865-78* (New York: Twayne Publishers, 1958), 17.

[2] Edward Ingle, *The Negro in the District of Columbia* (Baltimore, MD: Johns Hopkins University Press, 1893), 91; Whyte, *The Uncivil War*, 21, 31, 106, 178-79, 251, 257; Judith Beck Helm, *Tenleytown, D. C.: Country Village into City Neighborhood* (Washington, DC: Tennally Press, 1981), 168; Louise Daniel Hutchinson, *The Anacostia Story: 1608-1930* (Washington, DC: Published for the Anacostia Neighborhood Museum of the Smithsonian Institution by the Smithsonian Institution Press, 1977), 70; Oliver Otis Howard, *Autobiography of Oliver Otis Howard Major General United States Army*, Two Volumes (New York: The Baker & Taylor Company, 1908), volume 2, page 460.

[3] Patricia L. Faust, "Freedmen's Bureau," in *Historical Times Illustrated Encyclopedia of the Civil War*. (New York: Harper & Row, Publishers, 1986),. 290; Bobbi Schildt, "Freedman's Village," *Northern Virginia Heritage*, 7 (February 1985), 12; *Free at Last: A Documentary History of Slavery, Freedom and the Civil War*, Edited by Ira Berlin, Barbara J. Fields, Steven F. Miller, Joseph P. Reidy, and Leslie S. Rowland, Reprint Edition (Edison, NJ: The Blue & Gray Press, 1997),xxxiii, 331; Elaine Cutler Everly, "The Freedmen's Bureau in the National Capital," Ph.D. dissertation, George Washington University, 1972.

[4] Schildt, "Freedmen's Village," 11-12; University of Maryland, Freedmen and Southern Society Project, Xeroxed Documents Collection, J47; E.H. Luddington to Inspector General, Army; RG92, Consolidated Correspondence File, "Alexandria, Va," Box 22, DC area, March 1867, Capt S.F. Lee to Lt. W.W. Rogers, March 21, 1867; RG 105, District of Columbia, AC, Entry 456, Letters Received, S.N. Clark to W.W. Rogers, 10 Nov 1866, Box 3, #130, 9792; Eilliam Hazaiah Williams, "The Negro in the District of Columbia during Reconstruction," *The Howard Review*, 1 (June 1924), 140; Whyte, *The Uncivil War*, 32-33; Everly, "The Freedmen's Bureau."

[5] The District of Columbia Bureau officers submitted numerous reports, found in the Bureau records in the National Archives and among the Xeroxed Documents Collection maintained by the Freedmen and Southern Society Project at the University of Maryland describing and documenting the living conditions of freedmen and other refugees in the city but none of those examined contained any information about squatters at forts; Whyte, *The Uncivil War*, page 15; Benjamin Franklin Cooling, III, *Symbol, Sword, and Shield: Defending Washington During the Civil War* Second Edition (Shippensburg, PA: White Mane Publishing Company, 1991), 238-39.

[6] George Alfred Townsend, *Washington, Outside and Inside. A Picture and A Narrative of the Origin, Growth, Excellences, Abuses, Beauties, and Personages of Our Governing City* (Hartford, CT: James Betts & Co., 1873), 219-20.

[7] Townsend, *Washington, Outside and Inside.*, 640-41.

[8] Whyte, *The Uncivil War*, 15.

[9] Helm, *Tenleytown, D. C.*, 168; Louana M. Lackey, "A Preliminary Archaeological and Historical Survey of A Portion of Fort Reno Park in Washington, D. C. Prepared by the Department of General Services of the District of Columbia." Washington, DC: The Potomac River Archeology Survey, American University, 1983, 5-7; Neil E.

Heyden, "The Fort Reno Community: The Conversion and Its Causes. Washington, DC: Department of History, American University, 1981, 1-2.

[10] Helm, *Tenleytown, D. C.*, 168, 173-74; Lackey, "A Preliminary Archaeological and Historical Survey," 7; Heyden, "The Fort Reno Community," 1-2.

[11] Anne C. Webb, "Fort Strong on Arlington Heights," *Arlington Historical Magazine*, 5 (October 1973), 39; Anne Ciprani Webb, "Fort Strong on Arlington Heights," *Periodical: The Journal of the Council on Abandoned Military Posts*, 4, July 1972, 6; John. L. Viven, 1st Lt., 12th US Infantry, Acting Garrison Quartermaster, to Lt. Will A. Coulter, 12th U.S. Infantry, Garrison Adjutant, Washington, DC, RG393, PI 172, Pt. 1, Department and Defenses of Washington and 22nd Army Corps, 1862-69, E-5382, Letters Received, September 1862-March 1869, 8 W 1867, August [27 or 28], 1867; Special Order 54, Headquarters, Department of Washington, March 15, 1866; IV., RG92, Entry 225, Consolidated Correspondence File, "Fort Reno, D.C., 1863—, Box 892; *Army and Navy Journal*, 3 (March 24, 1866), 486; *Statutes at Large*, 38th Congress, 1863-65, Vol. 13 (Boston: Little Brown & Co., 1866), July 2, 1864, Chapt. CCXI, An Act making Appropriation For the Construction, Preservation, and Repairs of certain Fortifications for Year ending the 30th of June, 1865 . . ., 353-54; *Statutes at Large*, 38th Congress, 1863-65, Vol. 13 (Boston: Little Brown & Co., 1866), February 28, 1865, Chapt. LXVIII, An Act making Appropriations for the Construction, Preservation, and Repairs of certain Fortifications for Year ending the 30th of June, 1866 . . ., 442-43; Helm, *Tenleytown*, 168; RG393, PI 172, Pt. 1, Department and Defenses of Washington and 22nd Army Corps, 1862-69, Entry 5395, Station Book of Troops, 1866-68, Volume 59/73 DW, various returns; RG393, PI 172, Pt. 1, Department and Defenses of Washington and 22nd Army Corps, 1862-69, Entry 5375, Volume 5 of 5, Vol. 24, Letters Sent, Department of Washington, 1866-69, page 229, Assistant Adjutant General to General J.C. McFerrar, Oct 15, 1867, page 396, Acting Assistant Adjutant General Stacy to George W. Wallace, 12th US Infantry, Commanding Garrison, Washington, DC, Aug 18, 1868, and page 429, Oct. 3, 1868; RG393, PI 172, Pt. 1, Department and Defenses of Washington and 22nd Army Corps, 1862-69, Entry 5381, Registers of Letters Received, September 1862-March 1869, Volume 18 DW, August 1868, Guard at forts Corcoran, Greble & Strong; RG 393, PI 172, Pt. 1, Department and Defenses of Washington and 22nd Army Corps, 1862-69, Entry 5382, Letters Received, September 1862-March 1869, Lt. Col. Goe. W. Wallace, 12th US Infantry, Commanding Garrison of Washington, Washington, .DC to Bvt. Col. J.H. Taylor, Assistant Adjutant General, Department of Washington, 131 W 1868, Sept. 22, 1868; RG393, PI 172, Pt. 1, Department and Defenses of Washington and 22nd Army Corps, 1862-69, Entry 5382, Letters Received, September 1862-March 1869, Bvt. Major R.C. Parker, Capt. 12th Infantry, Commanding Post, Russell Barracks, Washington, DC, 28 R 1868, Sept 30, 1868; RG393, PI 172, Pt. 1, Department and Defenses of Washington and 22nd Army Corps, 1862-69, Entry 5382, Letters Received, September 1862-March 1869, E.D. Townsend, Assistant Adjutant General, Adjutant General's Office, to Bvt. Maj. Gen. W.H. Emory, Commanding, Department of Washington, Washington, DC, 82 A 1868, March 14, 1868; RG393, PI 172, Pt. 1, Department and Defenses of Washington and 22nd Army Corps, 1862-69, Entry 5382, Letters Received, September 1862-March 1869, E.D. Townsend, Assistant Adjutant General, Adjutant General's Office, Washington, DC, to Commanding General, Department of Washington, Through Headquarters, Military Division of the Atlantic, Washington, DC, 300 A 1868, August 13, 1868; RG393, P.I. 172, Pt. 2, Defenses of Washington, August 1865-April 1866, Entry 698, Special Orders and General Orders, August 1865-April 1866, Volume 248/612 DW, Headquarters, Defenses of Washington page 36, Special Order No. 61, Nov. 11, 1865; RG393, P.I. 172, Pt. 1, Department and Defenses of Washington and 22nd Army Corps, 1862-69, Entry 5376, Letters Sent, Supplemental, 1866-69, Vol. 25/31 DW, page 50, JA Hopkins, Chief of Artillery to G.A. DeRussy, Chief of Artillery, Commanding Division, April 13, 1865, page 62, JA Haskins to M.D.

Hardin, Commdg Division, June 12, 1865, and page 63, J.A. Haskins to G.A. DeRussy, June 12, 1865; RG77, Entry 18, Letters Received, 1826-1866, B.S. Alexander to R. Delafield, A2331, Oct 18, 1865.

[12] RG 77, Entry 18, Letters Received, 1826-66, B.S. Alexander to R. Delafield; A2395, December 12, 1865; "The Dismantled Forts," *The Evening Star*, Thursday, Sept. 28, 1865; RG77, Entry 18, Letters Received, 1826-66, B.S. Alexander to R. Delafield, A2326, Oct. 17, 1865; RG77, Entry 18, Letters Received, 1826-66, B.S. Alexander to R. Delafield, A2363, Nov 25, 1865; RG77, Entry 18, Letters Received, 1826-66, B.S.Alexander to R. Delafield, A2379, Dec. 5, 1865; RG77, E-18, Letters Received, 1826-66, B.S. Alexander to R. Delafield, A2395, Dec. 12, 1865; RG77, Entry 30, Letters Sent, Third Division, Volume 2, page 527, J.D. Kurtz (OCE) to N. Michler, April 20, 1869: RG77, Entry 18, Letters Received, 1826-66, B.S. Alexander to R. Delafield, A2191, June 5, 1865; Cooling, *Symbol, Sword and Shield*, 233; Record Group 77, E-36, Letters Received ("A" File), November 1867-November 1870, Bvt. Major W.K. King to Gen. J.H. Simpson, A1173, Received July 20, 1868. ; Anne Ciprani Webb, "Fort Strong on Arlington Heights,"*Periodical*, 6; Special Order 54, Headquarters, Department of Washington., March 15, 1866; IV., RG92, Entry 225, Consolidated Correspondence File, "Fort Reno, D.C., 1863—," Box 892; Special Order No. 533, Headquarrters of the Army, Adjutant General's Office, Washington, DC, October 9, 1865; 4; RG77, E-36, Letters Received ("A" File), November 1867-November 1870, Bvt Brig. Gen. N. Michler, Office of Public Buildings, Grounds, and Works, U.S. Capitol, Washington, DC, to Chief of Engineers, A2284, May 8, 1869; RG77, E-36, Letters Received ("A" File), November 1867-November 1870, Bvt Maj. W.R. King, July 2, 1868, Letter Sent to Gen. James H. Simpson, A1173, July 2, 1868; RG92, Consolidated Correspondence File, "Alexandria, Va," Box 22, DC area, March 1867, Capt S.F. Lee to Lt. W.W. Rogers, March 21, 1867; *Army and Navy Journal*, November 25, 1865, page 208; Anne C. Webb, "Fort Strong on Arlington Heights," *Arlington*, 39; RG393, PI 172, Pt. 1, Department and Defenses of Washington and 22nd Army Corps, 1862-69, Entry 5382, Letters Received, September 1862-March 1869, E.D. Townsend, Assistant Adjutant General, Adjutant General's Office, to Bvt. Maj. Gen. W.H. Emory, Commanding, Department of Washington, Washington, DC, 82 A 1868, March 14, 1868; RG393, PI 172, Pt. 1, Department and Defenses of Washington and 22nd Army Corps, 1862-69, Entry 5375, Letters Sent, 1864-69, Volume 23 DW, page 440, Acting Assistant Adjutant General to J.A. Haskin, April 18, 1866; RG393, Department and Defenses of Washington and 22nd Army Corps, 1862-69, Entry 5421, Letters Sent, 1865-69 & Entry 5422, Endorsements Sent, 1865-69, volume 79 DW, page 29, J.B. Campbell to Bvt. Col. D.M. Sells, Commanding 107 U.S. Colored Troops, October 19, 1866

[13] RG393, PI 172, Pt. 1, Department and Defenses of Washington and 22nd Army Corps, E-5382, Letters Received, September 1862-March 1869, John L. Viven, 1st Lt., 12 US Infantry, Acting Garrison Quartermaster, to Lt. Will A. Coulter, 12th U.S. Infantry, Garrison Adjutant, Washington, DC, 8 W 1867, August [27 or 28], 1867; Special Order 54, Headquarters, Department of Washington., March 15, 1866; IV., RG92, Entry 225, Consolated Correspondence File, "Fort Reno, D.C., 1863—," Box 892; RG393, PI 172, Pt. 1, Department and Defenses of Washington and 22nd Army Corps, 1862-69, E-5382, Letters Received, September 1862-March 1869, E.D. Townsend, Assistant Adjutant General, Adjutant General's Office, to Bvt. Maj. Gen. W.H. Emory, Commanding, Department of Washington, Washington, DC, 82 A 1868, March 14, 1868; *The Army and Navy Journal*, 2 (November 25, 1865), 208.

[14] RG393, PI 172, Pt. 1, Department and Defenses of Washington and 22nd Army Corps, 1862-69, Entry 5375, Vol 5 of 5, Vol. 24, Letters Sent, Department of Washington, 1866-69, page 187, Aug. 29, 1867, General Commanding Department to General A.B. Dyer, Ordnance Department; National Archives Microfilm Pub., M617, Post Returns, Post Return, Fort Greble, DC, Roll 1378, October, 1867; *Army and Navy Journal*, Volume 3, March 24, 1866, 486.

15 Benjamin Franklin Cooling, III and Walton H. Owen, II, *Mr. Lincoln's Forts: A Guide to the Civil War Defenses of Washington* (Shippensburg, PA: White Mane Publishing Company, 1988), 215; Jacqui Handly, *Civil War Defenses of Washington, D.C.: A Cultural Landscape Inventory* (Washington, D.C.: The Government Printing Office, Falls Church Office, Denver Service Center, National Park Service], 1996), 45; George J. Olszewski, *Historic Structures Report: Forts Carroll and Greble, Washington, D.C.* (Washington, DC: Office of History and Historic Architecture, Eastern Service Center, National Park Service, 1970), 24; RG393, PI 172, Pt. 1, Department and Defenses of Washington and 22nd Army Corps, 1862-69, Entry 5381, Registers of Letters Received, September 1862-March 1869, Volume 18 DW, Albert J. Myer Meyer request Fort Greble, August 12, 1868; Rebecca Robbins Raines. *"Getting the Message Through": A Branch History of the U.S. Army Signal Corps Army Historical Series* (Washington, DC: The Government Printing Office, 1996), 43-44; Paul J. Scheips, "'Old Probabilities': A.J. Myer and the Signal Corps Weather Service," *The Arlington Historical Magazine*, 5 (October 1974), 31; RG393, PI 172, Pt. 1, Department and Defenses of Washington and 22nd Army Corps, 1862-69, Entry 5382, Letters Received, September 1862-March 1869, J.C. Kelton, Asst. Adj. Gen., War Department, to the Commanding General, Department of Washington, through Headquarters Military Division of the Atlantic, Washington, DC., Washington, D.C., 107 W 1868 August 20, 1868.

16 RG77, Entry 18, Letters Received, 1826-66, B.S. Alexander to R. Delafield, A2379, Dec. 5, 1865; RG77, E-18, Letters Received, 1826-66, B.S. Alexander to R. Delafield, A2395, Dec. 12, 1865; RG77, E-18, Letters Received, 1826-66, B.S. Alexander to R. Delafield, A2363, Nov 25, 1865; RG77, E-36, Letters Received ("A" File), November 1867-November 1870, T.J. Treadwell, Ordnance Department to Chief of Engineers, A2190, April 14, 1869; RG77, E-36, Letters Received ("A" File), November 1867-November 1870, T.J. Treadwell, Ordnance Department to Chief of Engineers, A2205, April 19, 1869; RG77, E-36, Letters Received ("A" File), November 1867-November 1870, W.P. Craighill, Engineer Office, Baltimore, MD, to Ch. Of Engineers, A3624, May 13, 1870; RG77, E-36, Letters Received ("A" File), November 1867-November 1870, Mr. Samuel O. Bagot to W.P. Craighill, A-3557, April 20, 1870; R G77, E-36, Letters Received ("A" File), November 1867-November 1870, W.P. Craighill, Engineer Office, Baltimore, MD, to Chief of Engineers, A3624, April 28, 1870; RG77, E-36, Letters Received ("A" File), November 1867-November 1870, Adjutant General to Commanding General, 1st Military District, Richmond, Va., A10623, June 6, 1868; RG77, E-36, Letters Received ("A" File), November 1867-November 1870, Bvt Maj. W.R. King, A1173, July 2, 1868, Letter Sent to Gen. James H. Simpson, July 2, 1868; RG77, E-36, Letters Received ("A" File), November 1867-November 1870, Bvt. Brig. Gen. N. Michler, Office of Public Buildings, Grounds, and Works, U.S. Capitol, Washington, DC, to Chief of Engineers, A2284, May 8, 1869; *The Army and Navy Journal*, 2 (November 25, 1865), 208, and 3 (March 24, 1866), 486; RG393, Department and Defenses of Washington and 22nd Army Corps, 1862-69, Entry 5421, Letters Sent, 1865-69 & Entry 5422, Endorsements Sent, 1865-69, volume 79/126 & 127 DW, page 29, J.B. Campbell to Bvt. Col. D.M. Sells, Commanding. 107 US Colored Troops, October 19, 1866; RG77, Entry 30, Letters Sent, 1866-70, Volume 3, 1869-70, 1st Division, .Page 18, N. Michler, June 24, 1869; Special Order 54, Headquarters, Department of Washington., March 15, 1866; IV., RG92, Entry 225, Consolidated Correspondence File, "Fort Reno, D.C., 1863— ," Box 892; RG393, P.I. 172, Pt. 1, Department and Defenses of Washington and 22nd Army Corps, 1862-69, Entry 5375, Letters Sent, July 1864-March 1869, Volume 23 DW, Page 440, Acting Assistant Adjutant General, Department of Washington to J.A. Haskins, April 18, 1866; RG393, Department and Defenses of Washington and 22nd Army Corps, 1865-69, Entry 5421, Letters Sent, 1865-69 & Entry 5422, Endorsements Sent, 1865-69, volume 79/126 & 127 DW, page 29, J.B. Campbell to Bvt. Col. D.M. Sells, Commanding. 107 US Colored Troops, October 19, 1866; Cooling, *Symbol, Sword and Shield*, 233; RG 77, Entry 36, Letters Received ("A" File), November 1867- November 1870, Bvt. Major W.K. King to Chief of Engineers, Sent to Gen. J.H. Simpson,

A1173, Received July 20, 1868; RG77, Entry 18, Letters Received, 1826-1866, B.S. Alexander to Delafield, A2326, Received Oct. 18, 1865,; Entry 18, Letters Received, 1826-1866, B.S. Alexander to R. Delafield, A2395, December 12, 1865,; RG393, PI 172, Pt. 1, Department and Defenses of Washington and 22nd Army Corps, 1862-69, E-5382, Letters Received, September 1862-March 1869, E.D. Townsend, Assistant Adjutant General, Adjutant General's Office, to Bvt. Maj. Gen. W.H. Emory, Commanding, Department of Washington, Washington, DC, 82 A 1868, March 14, 1868.

[17] RG393, PI 172, Pt. 1, Department and Defenses of Washington and 22nd Army Corps, Entry 5382, Letters Received, September 1862-March 1869, Bvt. Brig. Gen. F.T. Dent, ADC, by order of Secretary of War, to Gen. W.H. Emory, Commanding Department of Washington,, 285 W 1867, Nov. 23, 1867; RG393, PI 172, Pt. 1, Department and Defenses of Washington and 22nd Army Corps, Entry 5376, Letters Sent, Supplemental, 1866-69, Vol. 25/31 DW, page 76, July 17th, 1865; RG393, Department and Defenses of Washington and 22nd Army Corps, 1862-69, Entry 5421, Letters Sent, 1865-69 & Entry 5422, Endorsements Sent, 1865-69, volume 79/126 & 127 DW, page 29, J.B. Campbell to Bvt. Col. D.M. Sells, Commanding. 107 US Colored Troops, October 19, 1866; Leonard E. Brown, *National Capital Parks: Fort Stanton, Fort Foote, Battery Ricketts* (Washington, DC: Office of History and Historic Architecture, Eastern Service Center, National Park Service, 1970), 78 ; U.S., Army Corps of Engineers, Washington District, *A Historical Summary of the Works of the Corps of Engineers in Washington, DC and Vicinity 1852-1952* By Sacket L. Duryee (Washington, DC: U.S., U.S. Army Corps of Engineers, Washington District, 1952), 26; RG 94, E-464, Reservation File, "Fort Foote."

[18] *The Army and Navy Journal*, 3 (March 10, 1866), 454 and (March 24, 1866), 486; Anne Ciprani Webb, "Fort Strong on Arlington Heights," *Periodical*, 6.

[19] RG393, P.I. 172, Pt. 1, Department and Defenses of Washington and 22d Army Corps, 1862-69, Entry 5375, Letters Sent, 1864-69, volume 23 DW, page 210, Acting Assistant Adjutant General, Department of Washington, to J.A. Haskin, Commanding Defenses of Washington, Aug. 28, 1865 and page 410, Major General Commanding to J.A. Haskin, Commanding Defenses of Washington, March 7, 1866.

[20] RG77, E-36, Letters Received ("A" File), November 1867-November 1870, Bvt. Lt. Col. W.P. Craighill, Engineer Office, Baltimore, MD, to Chief of Engineers, A3624, April 28, 1870; Bvt. Lt. Col. W.P. Craighill, Baltimore, MD, to Chief of Engineers, A3602, May 4, 1870; Adjutant General to Commanding General, 1st Military District, Richmond, Va., A10623, June 6, 1868, furnished for the information of the Chief of Engineers, June 11, 1868;p Bvt. Lt. Col. W.P. Craighill, Baltimore, MD, to Chief of Engineers, A3694, June 9, 1870; Bvt. Lt. Col. W.P. Craighill, Baltimore, MD, to Chief of Engineers, A3779, July 4, 1870; Bvt. Lt. Col. W.P. Craighill, Baltimore, MD, to Chief of Engineers, A3909, July 10, 1870; Bvt. Lt. Col. W.P. Craighill, Baltimore, MD, to Chief. of Engineers, A3892, Aug 9, 1870; Bvt. Lt. Col. Craighill, Baltimore, MD, to Ch. Of Engineers, A4268, Nov 1, 1870; George W. Cullum, Z.B. Tower & Wm. P. Craighill, Office, Board of Engineers for Fortifications, Army Bldg, New York, to Chief of Engineers, A4320, Nov. 9, 1870; and Bvt. Lt. Col. W.P. Craighill, Baltimore, MD, to Chief of Engineers, A4354, Dec 1, 1870; T. Michael Miller, "Jones Point: Haven of History," The Historical Society of Fairfax County, Virginia *Yearbook*, 21 (1986-1988), 15-73; William J. Dickman, *Battery Rodgers at Alexandria, Virginia* (Manhattan, KS: MA/AH Publishing, 1980), 30.

[21] *Report of the Chief of Engineers Accompanying Report of Secretary of War, 1867* (Washington, DC: The Government Printing Office, 1870), 520; *Annual Report of the Chief of Engineers to the Secretary of War for the Year 1870* (Washington, DC: The Government Printing Office, 1870), 21; *Report of the Secretary of War, Being*

Part of the Message and Documents Communicated to the Two Houses of Congress at the Beginning of the Second Session of the Forty-Second Congress., House Executive Document 1, Part 2 (42d Congress, 2d Session) Volume II (Washington, DC: The Government Printing Office, 1871), 17-18; *Annual Report of the Chief of Engineers to the Secretary of War for the Year 1873, House Executive Document 1*, Part 2, Vol. II (Washington, DC: The Government Printing Office, 1873), 15; *Annual Report of the Chief of Engineers to the Secretary of War for the Year 1874, House Executive Document 1*, Part 2, Vol. II (Washington, DC: The Government Printing Office, 1874), 18; *Annual Report of the Chief of Engineers to the Secretary of War for the Year 1875, House Executive Document 1*, Part 2, Vol. II (Washington, DC: The Government Printing Office, 1875), 19; *Annual Report of the Chief of Engineers to the Secretary of War for the Year 1876, House Executive Document 1*, Part 2, Vol. II (Washington, DC: The Government Printing Office, 1876), 20; *Annual Report of the Chief of Engineers to the Secretary of War for the Year 1877, House Executive Document 1*, Part 2, Vol. II (Washington, DC: The Government Printing Office, 1877), 16; *Annual Report of the Chief of Engineers to the Secretary of War for the Year 1878, House Executive Document 1*, Part 2, Vol. II (Washington, DC: The Government Printing Office, 1878), 19; *Annual Report of the Chief of Engineers to the Secretary of War for the Year 1879, House Executive Document 1*, Part 2, Vol. II (Washington, DC: The Government Printing Office, 1879), 23; *Annual Report of the Chief of Engineers to the Secretary of War for the Year 1880, House Executive Document 1*, Part 2, Vol. II (Washington, DC: The Government Printing Office, 1880), 39; *Annual Report of the Chief of Engineers to the Secretary of War for the Year 1882, House Executive Document 1*, Part 2, Vol. II (Washington, DC: The Government Printing Office, 1882), 35-36, 421; *Annual Report of the Chief of Engineers to the Secretary of War for the Year 1882, House Executive Document 1*, Part 2, Vol. II (Washington, DC: The Government Printing Office, 1882), 35-36, 42; *Annual Report of the Chief of Engineers, United States Army, to the Secretary of War for the Year 1885, House Executive Document 1*, Part 2, Vol. II (Washington, DC: The Government Printing Office, 1885), 30; Brown, *Fort Stanton*, 51-129; *Surgeon General Circular No. 8, A Report on the Hygiene of the United States Army, with Descriptions of Military Posts* (Washington, DC: GPO, 1875), 24-25; RG 94, E-464, Reservation File, "Fort Foote"; RG393, PI 172, Pt. 1, Department and Defenses of Washington and 22nd Army Corps, Entry 5382, Letters Received, September 1862-March 1869, 121 F 1868; U.S., Army Corps of Engineers, Washington District, *A Historical Summary*, 25; RG77, Entry 171, Land Papers, 1794- 1916, District of Columbia; RG 393, PI 172, Pt. 1, Department and Defenses of Washington and 22nd Army Corps, Entry 5382, Letters Received, September 1862-March 1869, Bvt. Col. R. Losear (?), Capt., 4th US Arillery to Department Commander, 179 F 1867, Nov. 28, 1867; RG393, P.I. 172, Pt. 1, Department and Defenses of Washington and 22d Army Corps, 1862-69, Entry 5375, Letters Sent, 1864-69, volume 23 DW, pages 508-10, Major General commanding to the Chief of Staff, Army of the United States, August 30, 1866; RG393, PI 172, Pt. 1, Department and Defenses of Washington and 22nd Army Corps, 1862-69, Entry 5395, Station Book of Troops, 1866-68, Volume 59/73 DW, various dates; RG393, Department and Defenses of Washington and 22nd Army Corps, 1862-69, Entry 5421, Letters Sent, 1865-69 & Entry 5422, Endorsements Sent, 1865-69, volume 79/126 & 127 DW, page 28, J.B. Campbell, Acting Assistant Iinspector Gneral, to Bvt. Col. J.H. Taylor, AAG, Department Of Washington., Oct. 15, 1865; RG77, E-18, Letters Received, 1826-66, B.S. Alexander to R. Delafield, A2260, Aug. 2, 1865; RG77, E-18, Letters Received, 1826-66, Report on 15-inch Gun at Ft. Foote, A2303, Sept. 16, 1865; Randolph Keim. *Keim's Illustrated Hand-Book. Washington and Its Environs: A Descriptive and Historical Hand-Book to the Capital of the United States of America* Fourth Edition, corrected to July, 1874 (Washington, DC: For the Compiler, 1874), 230.; Townsend, *Washington, Outside and Inside.*, 723; RG393, P.I. 172, Pt. 1, Department and Defenses of Washington and 22d Army Corps, 1862-69, Entry 5375, Letters Sent, 1864-69, Volume 23 DW, pages 508-10, Major General Commanding to the Chief of Staff, Army of the U.S., August 30, 1866; National Archives Microfilm Publication, M617, Post Returns, Fort Foote, MD, 1864-78, roll 370; RG77, E-36, Letters Received ("A" File), November 1867-November 1870, Barnard, New York, to Chief of Engineers, A3711, June 8, 1870; RG 77, E-36, Letters Received ("A" File), November 1867-November 1870, J.D. Kurtz, Lt. Col. Engineers, Bvt. Col., US Engineer Office, No.1930 Penn Ave, Washington, DC,, to Bvt Maj.Gen. A.A. Humphreys, Chief of Engineers, Washington, DC, A3412, March 2, 1870; RG77, E-36, Letters Received ("A" File), November 1867-November 1870, Bvt. Brig. Gen. N. Michler, Office of Public Buildings, Grounds, and Works, U.S. Capitol, Washington, DC, to Chief of Engineers, A2284, May 8, 1869; RG77, E-36, Letters Received ("A" File), November 1867-November 1870, Bvt. Lt. Col. Craighill, Baltimore, MD, to Chief of Engineers, A3602, May 4, 1870; RG77, E-36, Vol. 53 DW, Bvt. Lt. Col. Craighill, Baltimore, MD, to Chief of Engineers, A3694, June 9, 1870; RG77, E-36, Letters Received ("A" File), November 1867-November 1870, Bvt. Lt. Col. Craighill, Baltimore, MD, to Chief Of Engineers, A3779, July 4, 1870; RG77, E-36, Letters Received ("A" File), November 1867-November 1870, Bvt. Lt. Col. Craighill, Baltimore, MD, to Chief of Engineers, A3909, July 10, 1870; RG77, E-36, Letters Received ("A" File), November 1867-November 1870, Bvt. Lt. Col. Craighill, Baltimore, MD, to Chief of Engineers, A3892, Aug 9, 1870; RG77, E-36, Letters Received ("A" File), November 1867-November 1870, Bvt. Lt. Col. Craighill, Baltimore, MD, to Chief of Engineers, A4268, Nov 1, 1870; RG77, E-36, Letters Received ("A" File), November 1867-November 1870, George W. Cullum, Z.B. Tower & Wm. P. Craighill, Office Board of Engineers for Fortifications, Army Bldg, New York, to Chief of Engineers, A4320, Nov. 9, 1870; RG393, P.I. 172, Pt. 1, Department and Defenses of Washington and 22d Army Corps, 1862-69, Entry 5385, Volume 6 of 6, Volume 53 DW, General Order No. 62, Headquarters, Department of Washington, October 19, 1866; RG77, E-36, Letters Received ("A" File), November 1867-November 1870, Bvt. Brig. Gen. N. Michler, Office of Public Bldgs, Grounds, and Works, to Chief of Engineers, A1149, July 14, 1868; RG 393, P.I. 172, Pt. 1, Department and Defenses of Washington and 22d Army Corps, 1862-69, Entry 5386, General Orders and Circulars, 1867-69, volume 1 of 2, General Order No. 18, March 14th, 1867, Headquarters, Department Of Washington; RG393, P.I. 172, Pt. 1, Department and Defenses of Washington and 22d Army Corps, 1862-69, Entry E-5375, Letters Sent, July 1864-March 1869, Volume 23DW, pages 508-10, Major General Commanding to the Chielf of Staff, Army of the United States, August 30, 1866.

[22] Cooling, *Mr. Lincoln's Forts*, 232; Ed Fitzgerald to Rock Comstock, September 24, 1973, CRBIB Material, Fort Circle Parks, in Stephen Potter's Office, National Park Service, National Capital Parks; U.S., Army Corps of Engineers, Washington District. *A Historical Summary*, 25; Brown, *Fort Stanton* , 78, 92-94; RG 94, E-464, Reservation File, Fort Foote; *Annual Report of the Chief of Engineers to the Secretary of War for the Year 1879, House Executive Document 1*, Part 2, Vol. II (Washington, DC: The Government Printing Office, 1879), 23: *Annual Report of the Chief of Engineers to the Secretary of War for the Year 1880, House Executive Document 1*, Part 2, Vol. II (Washington, DC: The Government Printing Office, 1880), 39; *Annual Report of the Chief of Engineers to the Secretary of War for the Year 1882, House Executive Document 1,* Part 2, Vol. II (Washington, DC: The Government Printing Office, 1882), 35-36, 421; *Annual Report of the Chief of Engineers, United States Army, to the Secretary of War for the Year 1885, House Executive Document 1*, Part 2, Vol. II (Washington, DC: The Government Printing Office, 1885), 30; Martha Strayer,"Old Fort Foote, A Forlorn and Forgotten Place," *The Washington Daily News*, Monday, July 20, 1931.

[23] Cooling, *Mr. Lincoln's Forts*, 233; *Statutes at Large*, 38th Congress, 1863-65, Volume 13 [(Boston: Little Brown & Co., 1866), 354; RG77, E-36, Letters Received ("A" File), November 1867-November 1870, Chief of Engineers to Secretary of War, A1396, September 19, 1868; N. Michler to Chief of Engineers, A1386, August 1868; Bvt. Lt. Col. Craighill, Baltimore, MD, to Chief of Engineers, A3602, May 4, 1870; Bvt. Lt. Col. Craighill, Baltimore, MD, to Ch. Of Engrs, A3694, June 9, 1870; Bvt. Lt. Col.W.P. Craighill, Baltimore, MD, to Chief of Engineers, A3779, July 4, 1870; Bvt. Lt. Col. Craighill, Baltimore, MD, to Chief of Engineers, A3892, August 9, 1870; Bvt. Lt. Col. Craighill, Baltimore, MD, to Chief of Engineers, A4268, Nov 1, 1870; Bvt. Lt. Col. Craighill, Baltimore, MD, to Chief of

Engineers, A4354, Dec 1, 1870; Bvt BG N. Michler, Office of Public Bldgs, Grounds, and Works, to Chief of Engineers, A1149, July 14, 1868; *Report of the Secretary of War, Being Part of the Message and Documents Communicated to the Two Houses of Congress at the Beginning of the Second Session of the Forty-Second Congress., House Executive Document 1,* Part 2 (42d Congress, 2d Session) Volume II (Washington, DC: The Government Printing Office, 1871), 17-18; Brown, *Fort Stanton,* 119-21.

[24] *The Army and Navy Journal,* 3 (March 10, 1966), 454 and (March 24, 1966), 486; RG393, Department and Defenses of Washington and 22nd Army Corps, 1862-69, Entry 5421, Letters Sent, 1865-69 & Entry 5422, Endorsements Sent, 1865-69, volume 79/126 & 127 DW, page 37, J.B. Campbell, Acting Assistant Inspector General, to Bvt. Col. D.H. Taylor, February 28, 1867; U.S., War Department, *Report of the Secretary of War, with the Reports of Officers, for the Year 1869,* Accompanying Papers Abridged (Washington, DC: The Government Printing Office, 1869), 276-81; *Surgeon General Circular No. 8,* 94; National Archives Records Administration, Record Group 98 (now in Record Group 393), Fort Myer, VA, Administrative History and Records Listings Page; *A Narrative History of Fort Myer Virginia* (Falls Church, VA: Litho-Print Press, 1954?), 2-3; *The History of Fort Myer Virginia 100th anniversary Issue* (Special Centennial Edition of the *Fort Myer Post*) June 1963, 4, 6, 8; RG77, E 171, Land Papers, 1794-1916, District of Columbia; Raines, *Getting the Message Through,* 43-44; Scheips, Old Probabilities, 31.

[25] General Orders No. 56., Headquarters Department Of Washington, Twenty-Second Army Corps, April 26, 1865, In U.S., War Department, *The War of the Rebellion: A Compilation of the Official Records of the Union and Confederate Armies* (Washington, DC: The Government Printing Office, 1880-190), Serial 97, 962, 1299; General Orders No. 118, War Department., Adjutant General's Office, June 27, 1865, U.S., War Department, *The War of the Rebellion,* Serial 97, 1299; *The Army and Navy Journal,* 2 (August 5, 1865), 796 (August 12, 1865), 801; RG393, P.I. 172, Pt. 1, Department and Defenses of Washington and 22d Army Corps, 1862-69, Entry 5385, Volume 6 of 6, volume 53 DW, volume 6 of 6, General Order No. 17, Headquarters, Department of Washington, Washington, DC, April 27th, 1866 [CC Augur, Commanding]; RG393, Pt. 1, Department and Defenses of Washington and 22d Army Corps, 1862-69, Entry 5385, Volume 6 of 6, Volume 53 DW, volume 5 of 6, General Order No. 109, Headquarters, Department of East, Aug 5, 1865, 2d.

[26] Henry L. Abbot, "Biographical Memoir of John Gross Barnard.' *Professional Memoirs, Corps of Engineers, United States Army and Engineer Department at Large,* 5 (January-February 1913), 83- 90; Robert G. Kindmark, "John Gross Barnard: His Civil War Career and Military Writings," Senior Paper, Allegheny College, April 1978; RG77, Entry 36, Letters Received ("A" File), November 1867-November 1870, J.G. Barnard, New York, to Chief of Engineers, A3335, March 28, 1870; John G. Barnard, *A Report on the Defenses of Washington, to the Chief of Engineers, U. S. Army, Corps of Engineers, Corps of Engineers Professional Paper No. 20* (Washington, DC: The Government Printing Office, 1871).

[27] Jubal A. Early,"General Barnard's Report on the Defences of Washington, in July 1864," *Southern Magazine* (Baltimore), 10 (June 1872), 724; RG77, Entry 36, Letters Received ("A" File), November 1867-November 1870, J.G. Barnard to Chief of Engineers, A1840, January 20, 1869; J.G. Barnard to J.D. Kurtz, A2987, November 11, 1869; J.G. Barnard, New York, to Chief of Engineers, A3335, March 28, 1870; J.G. Barnard, New York, to Chief of Engineers, A3544, April 11, 1870; J.G. Barnard, New York, to Chief of Engineers, A3711, June 8, 1870; J.G. Barnard, New York, to Chief of Engineers, A3758, June 27, 1870; Record Group 77, Entry 30, Letters Sent, 1866-70, Volume 2, Third Division, page 429, to J.G. Barnard, Jan.25, 1869; John G. Barnard, *A Report on the Defenses of*

Washington, to the Chief of Engineers, U. S. Army, Corps of Engineers, Corps of Engineers Professional Paper No. 20 (Washington, DC: The Government Printing Office, 1871).

[28] RG 77, Entry 103, General Correspondence, 1894-1923, #14394.

[29] John B. Ellis, *Sights and Secrets of the National Capital; A Work Descriptive of Washington and All Its Phases* (Chicago, IL: Jones, Junkin and Company, 1869), 22-23.

[30] *A Guide to the City of Washington, What To See, and How To See It* (Washington, DC: Philip & Solomons, 1869), 25-26.

[31] Townsend, *Washington, Outside and Inside*, 219.

[32] Townsend, *Washington, Outside and Inside*, 220.

[33] Townsend, *Washington, Outside and Inside*, 638.

[34] Townsend, *Washington, Outside and Inside*, 640-41.

[35] Townsend, *Washington, Outside and Inside*, 722-23.

[36] Townsend, *Washington, Outside and Inside*, 723.

[37] Mary Clemmer Ames, *Ten Years in Washington: Life and Scenes in the National Capital, as A Woman Sees Them* (Hartford, CT: A.D. Worthington & Co., 1873), 75.

[38] Keim, *Keim's Illustrated Hand-Book*, 232-33.

[39] Stilson Hutchins and W.F. Morse, *A Souvenir of the Federal Capital and of the National Drill and Encampment at Washington, D.C. May 23d to May 30th. 1887* (Washington, DC: W.F. Morse, 1887), 62.

[40] William H. Beach, *The First New York Lincoln (Cavalry) from April 19, 1861 to July 7, 1865* (New York: The Lincoln Cavalry Association, 1902), 523.

[41] RG46, 56th Congress, Committee Papers, Committee on Military Affairs, Sen 56A-F21, Box 97; Archives of the District of Columbia, Records of the District of Columbia, Central Classified Files: Engineer Department, (ED) Engineer Department Case Files, 1897-1955, #23181.

[42] U.S., Congress, Senate. *The Improvement of the Park System of the District of Columbia, Senate Report No. 166*, Edited by Charles Moore, 57th Congress, 1st Session (Washington, D.C.: The Government Printing Office, 1902), 11-12; U.S., Congress, Senate, Committee on the District of Columbia. *Park Improvement Papers: A Series of Twenty Papers Relating to the Improvement of Park System of the District of Columbia, No. 4, Fort Stevens, Where Lincoln Was Under Fire* by William V. Cox (Washington, D.C.: The Government Printing Office, 1901),17-25; "For Park At Fort Stevens," *The Washington Post*, December 21, 1906; "Fort Stevens," *The Washington Star*, March 27,

1911; Pamphlet, *Commemoration Ceremony on The One Hundreth Anniversary of the Battle of Fort Stevens at Fort Stevens* (Washington, D.C. , July 11, 1864).

[43] Rock Creek Park Files, Fort Stevens: Enabling Legislation,"Fort Stevens Property, Washington, D.C., Rock Creek Park Files, Fort Stevens: Enabling Legislation, S. 8142, 62d Congress, 3d Session, January 16, 1913; "Fort Stevens-Lincoln National Military Park," *Senate Document No. 433*, 57th Congress, 1st Session, June 26, 1902 (Washington, DC: The Government Printing Office, 1902); RG46, 59th Cong, Sen 59A-E1, Box 45; "For Military Park," *The Evening Star*, Thursday, December 20, 1906; "Fort Stevens, Near Washington City," *Confederate Veteran*, 8 (December 1900), 538; RG46, 56th Congress, Committee Papers, Committee on Military Affairs, Sen 56A-F21, Box 97; Archives of the District of Columbia, Records of the District of Columbia, Central Classified Files: Engineer Department, (ED) Engineer Department Case Files, 1897-1955, #23181; *Journal of the Senate of the United States* . . . 56th Congress, 2d Session (Washington, DC: The Government Printing Office, 1901), 247 (S6065); *Journal of the House of Representatives of the United States* . . . 57th Congress, 1st Session, 1901-02 (Washington, DC: The Government Printing Office, 1902), 290 (HR 10528); *Journal of the Senate of the United States* . . . 57th Congress, 1st Session, 1901-02 (Washington, DC: The Government Printing Office, 1902), 228, 521, 527 (S4476); *Journal of the Senate of the United States* . . . 58th Congress, 2d Session (Washington, DC: The Government Printing Office, 1903), 30, 47 (S2526); *Journal of the House of Representatives of the United States* . . . 58th Congress, 3d session, 1904-05 (Washington, DC: The Government Printing Office, 1905), 455 (HR19204); *Journal of the Senate of the United States* . . . 59th Congress, 1st Session, 1905-06 (Washington, DC: The Government Printing Office, 1906), 525, 547 (S6265); *Journal of the Senate of the United States* . . . 62d Congress, 3rd Session (Washington, DC: The Government Printing Office, 1912), 70 (S8142).

[44] "Fort Stevens," Editorial in *The Washington Star*, March 27, 1911; "Old Fort Stevens Sold, Purchased by Syndicate of Virginia and Maryland Capitalists": *The Evening Star*, March 22, 1911; "For Military Park," *The Evening Star*, Thursday, December 20, 1906;. "Fort Stevens, Near Washington City," *Confederate Veteran*, 8 (December 1900), 538.

[45] RG46, 59th Congress, Sen 59A-E1, Box 54 and 60th Congress, Sen 60A-E1, Box 36; "Public Park at Fort Thayer, District of Columbia," *Senate Report No. 362*, 60th Cong., 1st Sess. (Washington, DC: The Government Printing Office, 1908); *Journal of the Senate of the United States* . . . 59th Congress, 2d Session (Washington, DC: The Government Printing Office, 1907), 91 (S7646): *Journal of the Senate of the United States* . . . 60th Congress, 1st Session (Washington, DC: The Government Printing Office, 1908), 216 (S5132); *Journal of the House of Representatives of the United States* . . . 1907-08, 60th Congress, 1st Session (Washington, DC: The Government Printing Office, 1908), 526 (HR18129).

[46] RG46, 58th Congress, Sen 58A-E1, Box 38; US, US Army Corps of Engineers, St. Louis District. "AAA Site Fort Reno, Washington, D.C., Project Number-CO3DCO48401, March 1997," 4.1.1 General Site History"; RG66, E-17, Project Files, 1910-52, Forts, Fort Reno—Water Tower; RG77, E-103, General Correspondence, 1894-1923, #22803, September 25, 1897; *Journal of the House of Representatives of the United States* . . . 58th Congress, 2d Session (Washington, DC: The Government Printing Office, 1904), 270 (HR 12149); *Journal of the House of Representatives of the United States* . . . 1907-08, 60th Congress, 1st Session (Washington, DC: The Government Printing Office, 1908), 16, (HR291); *Journal of the Senate of the United States* . . . 58th Congress, 2d Session (Washington, DC: The Government Printing Office, 1904), 119 (S3886).

[47] *Journal of the Senate of the United States . . .* 62 Congress, 2d Session (Washington, DC: The Government Printing Office, 1912), 75, 93, 107; *Statutes at Large*, 62d Congress, 1911-13, Vol. 37, Pt. 1, June 24, 1912—Ch. 182 (Washington, DC: The Government Printing Office, 1918), 178-79; John Nolen, Jr., Director of Planning, Memorandum to Mr. Wirth: Subject: Fort Dupont Park, June 5, 1937, "Fort Dupont Park,"535, Parks & Recreation, Planning Files, 1924-67, General Records, Records of the National Capital Planning Commission, Record Group 328.

[48] U.S., Congress, House of Representatives. *Investigations Into the Affairs of the District of Columbia, Hous Report No. 72*, 42nd Congress, 2d Session (Serial 1542) (Washington, DC: The Government Printing Office, 1872), 739.

[49] "The Fort Drive, Major Powell's Proposed Circuit of the War Time Defenses, Historic Remains About This City, How Washington Was Defended During the Rebellion, Memories of the War: The Proposition of Engineer Commissioner Powell to establish a new drive-way through the suburbs of Washington to be called "Fort Drive," *The Evening Star*, May 23, 1896; Whyte, *The Uncivil War*, 137-48; Regina D. Eliot, "The Fort Drive." *The Washingtonian*, November 1930, 18; Gene Hart Day, "Washington's Scenic Masterpiece—A Highway of Fort," *American Motorist*, (February 1933), 16-17, 32-33; Paul H. Caemmerer, *A Manual of the Origin and Development of Washington; Senate Document No. 178* (75th Congress, 3d Session) (Washington, DC: The Government Printing Office, 1939), 108, 111-12; U.S., National Capital Planning Commission. *Worthy of the Nation: The History of Planning for the National Capital*. Frederick Gutheim, Consultant (Washington, DC: Smithsonian Institution Press, 1977), 194-96; William Bushong, *Historic Resource Study: Rock Creek Park - District of Columbia* (Washington, DC: The Government Printing Office, 1990), 93-95, 102; Thomas Walton, "The 1901 McMillan Commission: Beaux Arts Plan for the Nation's Capital," Ph.D. dissertation, Catholic University, 1980, 138, 149; U.S., Congress, Senate, *The Improvement of the Park System of the District of Columbia*; 57th Congress, 1st Session, *Senate Report No. 166* Edited by Charles Moore (Washington, DC: The Government Printing Office, 1902), 111-12; Carey H. Brown, Engineer, to The Newspaper Information Service, 1322 New York Avenue, Washington, DC, May 4, 1927, RG328, Planning Files, 1924-67, 545-100, Fort Drive, Fort Drive #1, page 6; Civil War Round Table of the District of Columbia, "Washington Needs The Fort Memorial Freeway," Brochure (1953); T.S. Settle, Legal Authority for Acquisition of Land and Construction of the Fort to Fort Drive, in the District of Columbia, November 14-15, 1940; T.C. Jeffers, A Brief History of The Fort Drive - Evolution of Its Concept and Function, March 17, 1947; T.C. Jeffers, "The Fort Drive, A Chronological History of the More Important Actions and Events Relating Thereto," February 7, 1947; RG328, Planning Files, 1924-67, 545-100, Fort Drive, #2; Colonel William W. Harts to Brigadier General William M. Black, Chief of Engineers, Re: Fort Drive, June 12, 1917, RG328, Planning Files, 1924-67, 545-100, Fort Drive, #1; "Justification: The Fort Drive - Washington, D.C., Syllabus, Archives of the District of Columbia, Records of the District of Columbia, Central Classified Files: Engineer Department (ED), Case Files, 1897-1955, #248515.

[50] RG328, General Records, Planning Files, 1924-67, 545-100, Fort Drive, #2,T.S. Settle, Secretary, and Legal Advisor, National Capital Park and Planning Commission. "Legal Authority for Acquisition of Land and Construction of the Fort to Fort Drive, in the District of Columbia," November 14-15, 1940, 2.

[51] U.S., Congress, Senate. *The Improvement of the Park System of the District of Columbia, Senate Report No. 166*, Edited by Charles Moore, 57th Congress, 1st Session (Washington, D.C.: The Government Printing Office, 1902), 111-12.

Chapter III

The Fort Park System

Acquiring The Fort Parks and Fort Drive

Little relating to the preservation or acquisition of the Civil War Defenses of Washington or the construction of Fort Drive occurred during World War I. In 1917, Colonel William W. Hart, Army Engineer, did survey the two "Park Commission of 1901" proposed "routes connecting the Anacostia Water Park with Rock Creek Park" and observed the Civil War forts along the way. He reported their condition, including the fact that Fort Thayer was gone due to new construction. Activity continued at Fort Myer, VA, formerly Fort Whipple, and at Fort Foote, MD, both still owned by the Army. And soon after the end of World War I, interest was rekindled in the forts and the road that would connect them.[1]

On July 30, 1919, Colonel Clarence S. Ridley, Officer in Charge of the Office of Public Buildings and Grounds, wrote the Chief of Engineers on the subject of a "Proposed Bill for Parkway connecting Old Civil War Forts, District of Columbia." In the letter, Ridley stated that in thinking of the future Federal Park System in the Capital, "the time is ripe" to secure the necessary parkland before "it is too late" for a "proper layout and design and for economy." He thought that the "best way to secure the purpose desired" was to have Congress consider and approve the project. Further, Ridley thought that for "the future development of the city and more particularly its park system," a restudy is necessary of "the parkway system as proposed by the Park Commission in 1902 with a view to adapting it to present conditions brought about by the growth of the city since the plan was made and then to incorporate the result." He enclosed with the letter "a Bill designed to carry the above into effect." The Chief of Engineers and the Secretary of War approved the plan by Oct. 20, 1919 and sent the correspondence and the proposed bill, to the Board of Commissioners of the District of Columbia, along with a listing of the various forts and information about their location, condition, and availability.[2]

The Board of Commissioners acted upon the plan by initiating in the House of Representatives a bill, H.R. 10695 (see appendices), "to make the necessary survey and to prepare a plan of a proposed parkway to connect the old Civil War forts in the District of Columbia" for the purpose of preserving the sites of the old Civil War forts and to make them accessible to the public. The Commissioners also wrote:

> "The old Civil War Forts surrounding the city are not only points of interest but also include points from which some of the best views of the city can be obtained. A parkway connecting these points would form a most useful adjunct to the park system in the District; and with the great activity in building operations, the Commissioners are of the opinion that steps should be taken in the near future to purchase the necessary land. The proposed parkway would occupy, in the main, a high ridge providing a splendid view of the city and Potomac River, and would connect the larger parks of the District besides providing numerous small recreation places."[3]

Introduced on November 19, 1919, the bill authorized the Commissioners of the District of Columbia to make a survey and submit a plan to the Congress as soon as possible, with recommendations "together with cost." as to what land to buy "to provide a continuous parkway of suitable width connecting the sites of the following old forts — Greble, Carroll, B. Ricketts, Stanton, Wagner, Baker, Davis (U.S. owned), Dupont (U.S. owned), Chaplin, A Battery, Mahan, Bunker Hill, Totten, Slocum, Stevens, De Russey, Bayard, B. Kemble, B. Vermont (U.S. owned), B. Parrott." Congress was further authorized to appropriate $5,000 for the study. This bill took some time to work its way through the Senate, but it did pass over a year later; the House of Representatives nver passed a similar bill so the proposed legislation never became law.[4]

The Commissioners did not give up. They resubmitted bills to both the House (H.R. 8792) and the Senate (S. 4) in 1921, which included the same text. Again, they did not pass. The House entertained a new bill in 1922 (H.R. 8792) to no benefit. In late 1923, a similar bill (S.1340) was introduced in the Senate. Among other things, the bill added a fort, Fort Lincoln. This bill took some time to work its way through the Senate, but it passed over a year later.[5]

While the Commissioners of the District of Columbia were attempting to influence Congress to approve the fort parkway, others assisted their efforts. The Washington Board of Trade of the District of Columbia, at its meeting on October 21, 1919, had adopted a resolution that urged Congress "to provide for the immediate acquisition of . . . tracts of land in the District for Parks and recreation purposes" including for the "Fort Drive, and sites of forts from Sixteenth Street to the Anacostia River; estimated cost $740,000." and "Fort Drive and site of fort from Pennsylvania Avenue, South East, to and including Fort Stanton, Anacostia; estimated cost $56,000." Concurrently, various citizens of the District decided that a permanent agency to plan, acquire, and develop the city parks was needed. The American Civic Association (later the American Planning and Civic Association), helped form the Washington Committee of 100 on the Federal City. Chaired by Frederic A. Delano, the Committee conducted a study and, in early 1924' published a report setting forth its recommendations, which included establishing "a Fort Boulevard following the hills encircling the city and connecting the Civil War forts."[6]

The Committee of 100 influenced the introduction of a bill in the United States Congress, "Providing for a comprehensive development of the park and playground system of the National Capital." On June 6, 1924, Congress passed the legislation which created the National Capital Parks Commission (NCPC) to oversee the comprehensive development of the park system. The NCPC created a Planning Committee to "review the 1901 McMillan Report on parks and bring it up to date with existing conditions." One of the first projects studied by the NCPC was the Fort Drive. On March 3, 1925, NCPC received its first appropriation for land acquisition and began acquiring Civil War Defenses of Washington lands.[7]

The Commission accomplished very little, however, before another important change occurred. On April 30, 1926, Congress created the National Capital Park and Planning Commission (NCPPC), replacing the NCPC and enlarging the agency's duties. In proceeding to develop a comprehensive park plan, the Commission had several bills introduced in Congress, all of which were referred to the Committee on the District of Columbia. In March 1928, the committee held extensive hearings on the legislation, and some speakers, including U.S. Grant, III, Major Carey H. Brown and Charles W. Eliot, II, specifically discussed the Fort Drive.[8]

Similar bills and hearings led to the passage on May 29, 1930, of the Capper-Cramton Act. This Act probably did more for the acquisition of the fort parks and for securing the right-of-way for the Fort Drive than any other legislation. It provided $16,000,000 for the acquisition of land, including the forts and Fort Drive. It further provided that when Fort Foote was no longer required for military purposes, the Director Of Public Buildings and Public Parks of the National Capital would receive title to it, without cost, for administration and maintenance as a part of the said George Washington Memorial Parkway. Most of the fort parks and right-of-way lands for the Fort Drive were acquired under this law and its appropriations.[9]

Another important organizational change occurred on June 10, 1933 when the Office of Public Buildings and Public Parks was abolished. Its duties were transferred to the Office of National Parks, Buildings and Reservations, Department of the Interior, and eventually to the National Park Service which became responsible for the national park system, including parks in the District of Columbia.[10]

Planning the Fort Parks and Fort Drive

While the Government made these organizational changes, important events and activities pertaining to the Civil War Defenses of Washington fortifications and the Fort Drive were unfolding. Captain J.E. Wood, Assistant to the Engineer Commissioner, District of Columbia, recommended "the establishment of a Fort Boulevard" and suggested naming it the McMillan Drive, in honor of the late senator. Following the passage of the 1924 act creating the National Capital Parks Commission, the first fort land, at Fort Stevens, was acquired on October 15, 1925. Then, on April 11, 1927, the new National Capital Parks and Planning Commission acquired the first property, in the Shepherd Parkway section, for the Fort Drive. In between these two acquisitions, the National Capital Parks and Planning Commission decided, at meetings on June 18-19, 1926, that the Fort Drive would be a parkway, "not just widened streets." On November 18, 1927, the Commission also approved five major park projects; the fort drive was one of them. It appeared that the Fort Drive plan was well on its way to reality.[11]

The Fort Drive plans changed considerably in the 1920s due to the growth of the city and development occurring within it. Captain Wood, on March 10, 1924, wrote that Fort Drive "is thirty-nine miles in
length, passes practically all of the Civil War forts and connects most of the important public reservations"
improving it "in that a complete circuit is made passing through Potomac Park." Continuing, he declared
"All of the streets indicated (see the appendices for accompanying map) are in good condition for motor
travel" and "They form a pleasant drive no part of which is habitually congested." The National Capital Parks
and Planning Commission decided, in June 1926, that Fort Drive would be a parkway, not city streets. In
1926, U.S. Grant, III, then the Executive and Disbursing Officer of the Commission, wrote that the 9th
Street section of Fort Drive "will probably have a double roadway with narrow parking between the two."
In 1925, J.C. Langdon, City Planner, offered a detailed Fort Drive project to the Commission which recommended a minimum parkway width of 140 feet and "negotiations were begun with the land holders," who
mostly requested inflated prices. After Major Carey H. Brown revised Langdon's scheme in July 1926, the
Commission authorized purchase within 125% or condemnation to widen Madison Street to 120 feet between building lines and recommended a special treatment of the street to give it as much parkway character
as possible." Charles W. Eliot, II, submitted a comprehensive report on Fort Drive to the Commission in
1927 "along the general line suggested by Langdon" with revisions made "to avoid new houses and improvements erected in the line" that provided "a satisfactory alignment and width of from 200 to 230 feet for a
parkway." This is the Fort Drive plan, with some subsequent minor changes, that the Government basically
followed until 1940. In May, Frederick Law Olmsted, II, advised Eliot to make a minor change after visiting
a particular section of Fort Drive but additional house construction negated that. On May 10, 1929, Eliot
submitted to Major Brown "three schemes for the location of the Fort Drive south of [Fort] Reno" recom-
mending Scheme A which was a parkway that would probably cost $58,993.[12]

The Government actually acquired most of the Fort Drive right-of-way between 1929 and 1932. In
March 1931, the National Capital Park and Planning Commission divided the plan and estimate of Fort
Drive into sections, for better management, so Section A was Potomac Ave. To Newark Street, Section H
was Randolph Street to Bladensburg Road (National Training School) and the last, Section P, was Atlantic
Avenue to Blue Plains. The Commission prepared an "Emergency Public Works Program Brief Justification
For Fort Drive Projects," on August 31, 1933 that listed each project by name, such as "Chesapeake St. to
Connecticut Ave." and "Madison Street to Fort Totten," that provided the planning stage, what type land it
was and expected use, and how much of the land was then in Government ownership.[13]

Some Fort Drive construction occurred in the 1930s. In 1934-35, Civilian Conservation Corps
(CCC) personnel, from the camp at Fort Dupont Park, graded Fort Drive toward Good Hope Road and to
Station 16, on the Anacostia connecting road. They also removed trees and roots from the Fort Drive right-

of-way. The Works Progress Administration constructed a section of Fort Drive in the Fort Reno area. In short, most Fort Drive road was completed during the Depression. [14]

In 1937, one newspaper reporter wrote that the 23 ½ mile-Fort Drive, with all but one mile purchased, would connect thirteen forts and four battery locations, of which the Government owned all but forts Chaplin and Greble and Battery Ricketts. But after 1936, the depression drastically cut funds for additional Fort Drive and fort land acquisition. On August 17, 1938 the Commissioners of the District of Columbia applied for $1,080,000. from the Public Works Administration (PWA) for Fort Drive construction, specifically the section from Conduit Road east to Fort Totten. To support the application, the National Capital Parks and Planning Commission prepared "General Specifications—Fort Drive Project," and "Justification: The Fort Drive—Washington, D.C. Syllabus." But, the PWA refused the request. [15]

Still optimistic, however, the National Capital Park and Planning Commission approved a complete set of 100 scale development plans for Fort Drive on September 30, 1932. The NCPPC prepared, in the Spring 1939, a "Statement Regarding Fort to Fort Drive Washington, D.C" that provided historical background, community needs, and immediate plans for the project including the announcement of a five year plan for its completion, constructing five miles each year. On November 16, 1940, the NCPPC, after trying for 13 years to "make a reality of Fort Drive," voted to press for a Congressional appropriation to begin construction of Fort Drive. Also in November 1940, the Commission approved the Downer plan, which embodied a limited access, four-lane divided parkway for passenger vehicles; this new Fort Drive plan supplanted the Eliot one that the Government had followed since 1929. The NCPPC had hired Jay Downer, an engineer consultant from New York, to develop a plan for completing Fort Drive as an outskirt bypass which would measurably relieve the downtown traffic problems. To develop this parkway, Downer reported that new standards and land acquisition, meaning a greater amount of right-of-way to accommodate wider roads, were necessary and recommended that the project be established as a 10-year plan. [16]

By late 1940, newspapers reported problems for Fort Drive. Worried Commissioners of the District of Columbia called for public hearings after Jay Downer estimated the Fort Drive's cost as high as $15,000,000.. It was stated that if the District of Columbia was forced to "pay the whole cost" of Fort Drive, there must be a rise in the gasoline tax. Realizing that some time might elapse before the road construction, the Office of Capital Parks rented out some of the right-of-way property, including a residence at 3125 Nebraska Avenue, N.W., for $80 per month. The Second World War then intervened, and most people forgot or ignored the issue of the Fort Drive. [17]

Acquisition and Development of Fort Parks

Meanwhile, many activities occurred over the first half of the Twentieth Century as the government began acquiring and developing the fort parks. Fort Dupont Park, authorized in 1912, received over 16 acres in 1916. After World War I, the park was expanded by acquisition and donation, mainly from financier, civic leader, philanthropist, American University trustee, and Corcoran Art Gallery president Charles Carroll Glover. Fort Dupont grew to become the second "largest natural park area in the city." The National Capital Parks and Planning Commission acquired approximately 2.8 acres for the "Fort Kemble" Park. It was almost fifteen years before the Government corrected the name (to Battery Kemble). At Fort Bayard Park, where the fortifications disappeared about 1910, developers were building homes. In 1923, the War Department offered Fort Foote for sale. Many people who felt it should become a park succeeded in forestalling the sale until Congress could reconsider its fate. The Capper-Cramton Act provided that Fort Foote would become a park after it no longer had a military purpose, and in 1940 the Army transferred it to the National Park Service. The Government had also acquired parts of Fort Stevens, although many houses surrounded it. A 1926 newspaper article reported that Fort De Russey, in Rock Creek Park, was about to be "restored and grassed," but that never happened.[18]

In the 1930s, the Civilian Conservation Corps (CCC) accomplished a great deal of work on the fort parks. The CCC established nine camps in the Washington, D.C. area, including one, established on October 23, 1933, at Fort Dupont Park. The CCC activities at Fort Dupont included erecting buildings for workers to live and eat in, cleaning up foot and horse trails, performing minor road construction, putting in a sewer, and constructing a two-car garage, carpenter shop, and toilet room. The CCC also performed "forest protection," including cleaning up dead and fallen lumber, burning brush, grubbing stumps, cleaning up the dump, and disposing of trash at forts Stanton, Bunker Hill and Mahan, and doing general cleanup at forts Totten and Foote. At Fort Stevens, the CCC undertook a restoration, reconstruction, and landscape project; costing $25,000. The workers rebuilt the western portion of the fort parapet, using cement "falsies," as one author called them, "instead of logs and planks," because they would last longer. The work at Fort Stevens was completed in 1938. It was the only fortification restoration project.[19]

With many of the forts and batteries back in Government possession, proposals for the placement of various non-park items on or around them were common. Water towers were proposed for Forts Reno, Dupont and Stanton. The City Board of Education suggested placing schools at various fort parks, including Forts Reno and Stanton. Plans were discussed for a new reservoir at Fort Reno and an incinerator at Fort Totten. A light, as aid to navigation, was mounted on the old wharf of Fort Foote, and the Aeronautics Authority wished to place a radio beam tower in the park. In 1931, parks office surveyors camped at Fort

Foote while surveying the "property on the Maryland side of the river which will be acquired as part of the George Washington Parkway." No one knew what might be proposed next.[20]

Fort Drive and the Parks After World War II

As during World War I, little of importance pertaining to Fort Drive and the fort parks occurred during World War II. The National Park Service and the District of Columbia signed a memorandum of agreement, on October 24, 1944, for the development of two Fort Drive sections, MacArthur Boulevard to Nebraska Avenue and Military Road from Oregon Avenue to a point east of 14th Street. National Park Service Associate Director A.E. Demaray informed the Secretary of the Interior that 98 percent of the Fort Drive right-of-way had been acquired and that its construction "is believed to be of first importance." He wrote that "the population recently has grown to the extent that the District Commissioners are prepared to undertake actual construction of certain sections." Demarary was a bit over optimistic, however, as the District of Columbia Engineer Commissioner, in 1946, argued that the estimated $32,000,000 cost for the drive was too high. The following year, estimating the cost of Fort Drive at $37,000,000, the District Commissioners cut off funding.[21]

In January 1947, the District Budget Officer and Assessor wrote a report, "Acquisition of Land," which basically stated that the Fort Drive was too costly and impractical or as they put it, "chimerical and useless." They declared that the project should be abrogated and the already acquired land sold. The same year, John Russell Young, President of the District's Board of Commissioners, argued that the "Fort Drive as planned would cost today about $35,000,000, which equals the sum total that we have available for major highway improvements for the next 12 years." The District, which at one time had considered raising the gasoline tax to obtain funds for the Fort Drive, now essentially abandoned the idea. In March 1947, Thomas C. Jeffers, Landscape Architect, presented a "modified plan for development of Fort Drive" which would cost less and use some of the existing streets and roads; the NCPPC approved a modified Fort Drive plan on June 20, 1947. The NCPPC and the National Park Service and the Commission on Fine Arts were still in favor of Fort Drive, but none of them had the money to build it. Interested groups, such as the Civil War Round Table of the District of Columbia, lobbied for the drive but, without a funding source, it did little good.[22]

Although supporters of the Fort Drive were unable to find funding after 1948, they continued to view it as a viable entity. In 1950, as the result of various studies, reports and meetings, a "Thoroughfare Plan" provided for portions of Fort Drive as express parkways and express highways. In 1959, plans proposed that portions of Fort Drive be incorporated into a newly planned intermediate loop roadway within

Washington, but still no new construction occurred. The District Highway Department, in 1961, attempted to take some of the unused Fort Drive right-of-way for Interstate 95, that would pass through the city but the National Park Service refused. In 1962, the National Park Service conducted a study of a Fort Drive "to decide whether it was still 'a valid park project' or should be built to serve as a major highway." In May 1963 President John F. Kennedy, in a message to Congress, requested the "speedy construction of the 23-mile Fort Drive Parkway" but his request went unfunded.[23]

On October 1, 1964, the National Capital Planning Commission staff and other professionals took a bus tour of Fort Drive to help decide whether it should "be developed as a park-like road, can it lend itself to be an intermediate loop, or should the forts remain isolated for just recreational use?" By May 1965 the local newspapers extolled a new proposal by Fred Tuemmler as a substitute for the Fort Drive. Tuemmler, whom the National Capital Planning Commission hired to re-evaluate Fort Drive, suggested the right-of-way land should "be reconstituted as a recreational facility" and, to emphasize that park recreation concept, rename it "Fort Park System." It would be "a place to get away from cars." Further, he saw it as a 30 mile "ring of recreation and green space" around the city, running from Fort Greble Park to Battery Kemble Park, with hiking and bicycle paths. He envisioned fully restoring Forts Stevens, Totten and Dupont. At Fort Totten Park, he suggested establishing a Civil War History Museum and adding 159.2 acres of land to the approximately 1,276 acres of existing parkland. All the forts, he said, would "serve as way stations, neighborhood centers and historical points of interest." As with the Fort Drive, lack of money halted Tuemmler's plan, but two miles of the hiking and biking trails were built in Fort Dupont Park.[24]

Over the years a concept evolved of a Fort Drive to run from MacArthur Boulevard in northwest Washington to Blue Plains at the District Line in the southeast. It would be "a quiet scenic road linking about 17 Civil War forts in the outer sections of Washington." A 1940 newspaper article reported that Fort Drive was "conceived now as a double strip roadway, free of grade crossings by which crosstown and through traffic may be accelerated and diverted around the more congested sections of the city." An engineer consultant called it "a miniature Penn[sylvania] turnpike with no traffic lights, two lanes divided by strip." A 1953 National Capital Parks study described it as "a high speed 'ring' road, distributing traffic on radial routes and handling circumferential traffic in the city." The same year, the Civil War Round Table of the District of Columbia saw it as a 22.8 mile, "six-lane freeway, with access only at selected points and no grade crossings when finally completed."[25]

In 1965, planning consultant Fred Tuemmler wrote: "Thus, the Fort Drive which started with a beginning concept of a 'wooded road—a picturesque circuit of the Capital' constituting 'the most striking feature of the park system' changed first to a design concept of which the Bronx River Parkway in Westchester

County, New York was the prototype and gradually to a more stream-lined facility to meet the design criteria of the present-day multi-laned, limited-access highway." He also observed that the Fort Drive evolved from a "meandering scenic drive to the recent concept as an indispensable encircling element in the system of high-speed traffic facilities devoted primarily to the movement of motor vehicles and with minor emphasis on the fort sites." In this sense, Tuemmler was right, a high-speed highway did not lend itself to sightseers who wished to stop and see the forts and the breathtaking views of the capital city.[26]

Advocates had a variety of justifications for the Fort Drive. An often used justification was: "Above all, it was the topographical value of the forts that was the most esteemed; that they ringed the city, defined its rim of surrounding hills, and (before trees had grown again and over the cleared lines of fire) offered such superb views of the city itself, the broad and gleaning Potomac, and the surrounding metropolitan landscape." The argument used in a 1919 bill introduced in Congress was: "For the purpose of preserving the sites of the old Civil War forts and to make them accessible to the public." In 1924, the District Commissioners were "of the opinion that as a matter of historic interest these forts should be preserved and that access to them should be provided before private development brings about their destruction." National Park Service Associate Director A.E. Demaray wrote that when the National Capital Park and Planning Commission, in 1926, "realized the necessity of providing a ready means for exchange of traffic between various residential subdivisions, fortunately, there was found a possibility for doing this at a moderate cost by a circumferential parkway about 23 miles in length joining the old Civil War forts." In 1947, the plea was that "to abandon the Fort Drive would be a short-sighted policy, it would destroy a 'cross town' traffic artery that is most urgently needed for the City of Washington."[27]

Although the arguments in favor of the road had merit, the opposition also had answers: "Unfortunately it will now be impracticable to carry out the fort drive on the scale proposed in 1901, as many sections of it have been built upon in the meantime" was an often repeated argument against it. Another retort was, "by 1926, the land required for the drive lay too close to the built-up city, so that the cost of this land would be much inflated over possible parkland further out." One author remarked that Fort Drive simply "never captured the imagination of Congress," which ultimately could have appropriated the money to acquire and build it. And, generally, although the road was "reinterpreted, even as a circumferential highway, the Fort Drive failed to win sufficient support to be realized." A 1964 newspaper article remarked that perhaps Fort Drive was no longer needed because, after all, city roads now ran past most of the forts. These arguments along with the lack of finances spelled doom for Fort Drive.[28]

Other Uses of the Fort Parks

While the Fort Drive was facing its demise, the fort parks were targets for various public and private entities. The Federal government has used Fort Reno Park, where the Civil War fortifications disappeared about 1900, for a variety of purposes, such as the previously mentioned water towers and reservoirs. During and after World War II, however, many new uses occurred. The military fenced the water facilities during the war to help prevent sabotage. During the Korean War, the 35th Brigade acquired 4.3 acres of the park for AAA Site Fort Reno by Department of Interior use permit of June 11, 1951. In September of 1952, Battery B of the 36th AAA Battalion (90 mm) and Battery A of the 70th AAA Battalion (120 mm) made their headquarters at Ft. Reno. After the truce, the use permit terminated on March 13, 1953. In two-week and weekend periods, the National Guard used the rolling fields at Fort Reno for drill and camp purposes during the Korean War. Soon after the war, the Government built an underground defense communications center there, with visible antennas and dishes, that "reportedly links the White House with other larger centers in the Middle Atlantic States."[29]

By 1957, Fort Reno Park had a new reservoir. The K-9 Division of the Secret Service also established a facility at the park. The City Department of Public Works stored sand, salt and other bad weather equipment, and the Federal Aviation Administration placed monitoring equipment there.[30]

Fort Reno was not the only fort park to experience these problems. The city wished to build a reservoir at Fort Totten and "run a 3-inch water main". . . across Fort Totten Park and Fort Drive to District water mains." In 1949, President Harry Truman submitted to Congress a "Supplemental Estimate of Appropriations for the Department of the Interior"requesting $175,000. for a swimming pool and associated facilities at Fort Stanton Park. Good or bad, at Fort Dupont, the buildings constructed and used by the CCC were offered to the park in 1944. Fort Foote was used by the Youth Conservation Corps in the mid-1980s. [31]

Non-government organizations also wished to use the fort parks. In 1920 African-American Catholics who had not felt comfortable in local congregations, built Our Lady of Perpetual Help Church at Fort Stanton, after Dr. J.C. Norwood, an African-American physician, reduced the price of the land. During the 1920s, nearby residents "walked family cows to Fort Stanton Park to graze before the school bell rang." Before World War II, the Girl Scouts used Fort Foote "for week-end recreation trips, camping out in a screened pavilion back of the old house where the flag flies." The Grand Army of the Republic (GAR) held national conventions in Washington in 1870, 1892, 1902, 1915, and 1936 and held special ceremonies at Fort Stevens, as did many other hereditary and patriotic organizations through the mid-1990s.[32]

While all these activities were occurring at the Civil War Defenses of Washington fort parks, all within the District of Columbia, one kindred fort, in Virginia, remained in the possession of the original owner's family and was well-preserved and seemingly safe until its sale in 1953. In 1954 Stan McClure, a National Park Service historian, recommended that the U.S. Government acquire this site, named Fort Marcy, "in connection with the land purchases along the George Washington Memorial Parkway." Despite the recommendation, nothing happened. In 1956, however, Virginia Highway Department proposals for widening Route 123 put Fort Marcy in jeopardy, and local preservationists spoke out for its protection. In June 1957 one of these individuals, Mrs. R.F.S. Starr, learned that the Virginia Highway Department was starting work at the fort. She contacted a Fairfax County Supervisor, drove to the site, and parked her car in front of the bulldozer's blade to halt further destruction. Later that day the County Supervisors voted to acquire the site and sent a police patrol to the site to insure that no additional destruction occurred. The County and the U.S. Government each paid half the cost for the site; ordinarily the State of Virginia would pay half the county's share, but a State Highway Department official indicated the state's stance by stating "I don't think we'd want to buy a Union fort." The Federal Government received the deed to the fort and surrounding land on May 7, 1959, but the park wasn't opened to the public until four years later, on May 18, 1963. Today, this 15 acre park is the site of the best preserved Civil War Defenses of Washington fortifications, containing not only a well-preserved fort but also related outworks and trenches. The park has suffered, however, from a lack of funds for preservation and interpretation. During the mid-1990s, the National Park Service conducted archaeological and geographical mapping work there, which has provided new historical insights into garrison life during the Civil War.[33]

Saving Non-Federally Owned Fortifications

In addition to the Federal government's efforts to save and preserve the Civil War Defenses of Washington, local governments have lately undertaken some of the work. National Park Service historian Stanley McClure wrote in 1954: "Expansion of residential and other building developments, beginning in 1942 after the outbreak of World War II, resulted in the destruction of several of the old fortifications preserved up to that time." But, he remarked, "The threatened destruction of the remaining earthworks has caused patriotic citizens and planning officials in Virginia and Maryland to take renewed interest in their preservation during the last several years." McClure then bragged: "As a result of the efforts taken to interest planning commissions and other organizations in the old Civil War earthworks during the past two years, and particularly in the last two months, it has been possible to aid in saving several others, including Fort Gaines, Battery Smead, Battery Bailey, Battery Benson, and probably Fort Ward."[34]

Of course, much has changed since 1954, and only two of those fortifications that McClure mentioned—Battery Bailey and Fort Ward—are preserved today and in public ownership.[35] At times, local governments and other organizations have attempted to save and preserve other fortifications, but with mixed results. They lost Fort Strong, Fort Worth, Fort Sumner, Fort Reynolds, and a great deal of Forts Scott and Ethan Allen. But Fairfax County was instrumental in saving Fort Marcy and paid part of its cost. In addition, Forts Ward, Willard and C.F. Smith and Battery Bailey are preserved, publicly owned and open to the public.[36]

Fort Ward may be the greatest success story. Preservationists made the Alexandria City government aware of Fort Ward in 1953 and voiced demands for its purchase and preservation. This influenced one writer to remark, "Fort Ward, which has been reconstructed, is the best example of an earthwork fort." By 1961, the city purchased the fort and surrounding land, approximately 40 acres. It then undertook a preservation and reconstruction plan, to make the northwest bastion appear as it did during the Civil War and to construct buildings patterned after those pictured in Matthew Brady photographs taken at the various forts in the Defenses of Washington. The park opened and was dedicated on May 30, 1964, during the Civil War Centennial. At times, the city has over-emphasized its recreational facilities and, as a result, interested individuals organized the Friends of Fort Ward to fight for the historical aspects of the park. With its reconstructed bastion, a museum with superior quality artifacts, an exemplary educational program, and a fine recreational facilities including an amphitheater, it is currently the premier Civil War Defenses of Washington fortification site in the Washington area.[37]

The next fort acquired by a local government was Fort Willard, in 1978-80. Located near Alexandria, VA, in Fairfax County, it contains 1.621 acres situated in the center of a cul-de-sac in the middle of a residential neighborhood. Civil War Historian James Robertson described the fort as "a superb example of an earthen fortification in an unimproved state." It retains most of its features, although physically protected only by barriers that prevent motor cycles and bicycles from riding through it. Few people know of it or its whereabouts, but it is an interesting fort to visit.[38]

Local governments have saved two other fortifications that were part of the Civil War Defenses of Washington — Battery Bailey, part of Little Falls Park in Montgomery County, MD, and Fort C.F. Smith in Arlington County, VA. Arlington County acquired Fort C.F. Smith in 1994, and it is a major part of a 19-acre public park, dedicated in 1996. Possibly, Fort C.F. Smith may be the last Civil War Defenses of Washington fortification in the suburbs to become a public park, because little else is left. Unable to save most of its Civil War fortifications, Arlington, in the mid-1960s, did spend $3,353. to place aluminum historical plaques at the sites of the 20 former Civil War forts in the county.[39]

Fort Parks - Still Relatively Unknown

Although a number of the Civil War Defenses of Washington have significant historical remains and warrant visits by interested tourists, the general guidebooks to the nation's capital have rarely mentioned them. These include the Federal Writer's Program's *Washington, D.C.: A Guide to the Nation's Capital*, originally published in 1942. Occasionally, Fort Stevens was cited and information provided about a few others. Even after the Government reacquired the forts for parks, few guidebooks discussed them. Below are a few of the better or more interesting guidebook accounts of the fortifications, taken from the limited selections that are available.[40]

- **"Some Forts of the Civil War**—At Brightwood, in plain view from the street cars on Georgia Ave., on the west are the crumbling parapets of **Fort Stevens**, the only battlefield in the district during the Civil War. Here was stayed the advance of the Confederate forces, and here Lincoln stood under fire during the attacks, repeatedly exposing himself to the fire of the sharpshooters. The site was marked by a memorial bowlder (sic!) in 1912, and was further marked in 1920, with a bronze tablet by the survivors of the Sixth Army Corps. In the little cemetery by the Methodist church, now known as Battle Cemetery were buried those killed in the attack.[41]

- "Fort De Russey is located on high ground northwest of the intersection of Military and Daniels Roads. The old dirt ramparts with their niches for artillery pieces are well preserved, and the old moat still surrounds the fort, although during the past sixty years many trees have grown up on the walls and in the fort proper."[42]

- 'Today, Fort Stevens is only a small open space with a flagpole, marker, and a few of the once numerous ramparts."[43]

- ' The extensive earthworks of Fort Sumner and Batgtery Benson will interest the history-minded pilgrim."[44]

Even today, few of the general Washington, D. C. guidebooks address the Civil War Defenses of Washington. The demand for information has grown, however, as Americans and many foreigners are increasingly visiting historical sites in the United States, especially those relating to the Civil War. So, in the last few decades, coverage of the Civil War Defenses of Washington in specific guidebooks has improved. Following are citations to the Civil War Defense of Washington fortification related guidebooks. David V. Miller's privately printed *The Defense of Washington During the Civil War* (Buffalo, New York: Mr. Copy, 1976) is the first modern guide to the Civil War Defenses of Washington. But the later published. *Mr.*

Lincoln's Forts: A Guide to the Civil War Defenses of Washington. (Shippensburg, PA: White Mane Publishing Company, 1988), by Benjamin Franklin Cooling, III and Walton H. Owen, II, is the best available at this time.

Other useful guides are Richard M. Lee, *Mr. Lincoln's City: An Illustrated Guide to the Civil War Sites of Washington* (McLean, VA: EPM Publications, Inc., 1981), Stephen M. Forman, *A Guide to Civil War Washington* (Washington, DC: Elliott & Clark Publishers, 1995), Charles T. Jacobs, *Civil War Guide to Montgomery County, Maryland* (Rockville, MD: The Montgomery County Historical Society and the Montgomery County Civil War Round Table, 1983) and James I. Robertson, Jr., *Civil War Sites in Virginia: A Tour Guide* (Charlottesville, VA: The University Press of Virginia, 1982).

Although many of the Civil War Defenses of Washington fortifications are gone or poorly preserved, their memory lives on in the commercial, educational, recreational, religious, transportation and residential activities of the nation's capital. Commercially, there is a Fort Carroll Delicatessen, Fort Davis Exxon, Fort Dupont Ice Rink, Fort Foote Computer Services, Fort Lincoln Beauty Boutique, Fort Stevens Liquor, Fort Totten Auto Sales, and Fort Worth Mortgage Corporation. Children can attend Fort Lincoln School or Fort Baker Kiddie Kollege. Those who wish, can attend Fort Baptist Church and/or be buried at Fort Lincoln Cemetery. One can live in Fort Greble Apartments, Fort Lincoln Senior Citizen's Village or Fort Ellsworth Condominium or on Fort Drive, Fort Williams Avenue, Fort Worth Place, Battery Heights Boulevard, or Fort Dupont Terrace. Or anyone can catch the Metro at Fort Totten Station or catch a bus that includes one of the former fort names in its final destination. Thus, although many of the fortifications in the Civil War Defenses of Washington are gone or in a terrible state of preservation, they live on, even today, in billboards, marquee and street signs.[45]

Endnotes

[1] Major General Amos A. Fries, Editor, "The District of Columbia in the World War," In John C. Proctor, Editor, *Washington, Past and Present: A History.* (New York: Lewis, 1930), 398-413; *A Narrative History of Fort Myer Virginia* (Falls Church, VA: Litho-Print Press, 1954?), 3; Ed Fitzgerald to Rock Comstock, September 24, 1973, CRBIB Material, Fort Circle Parks, in Stephen Potter's Office, National Park Service, National Capital Parks; Fort Foote," *The Evening Star*, June 1, 1926; Benjamin Franklin Cooling, III and Walton H. Owen, II. *Mr. Lincoln's Forts: A Guide to the Civil War Defenses of Washington* (Shippensburg, PA: White Mane Publishing Company, 1988), 232; Record Group 328, Records of the National Capital Planning Commission, National Archives (hereafter referred to as RG328), General Records, Planning Files, 1924-67, 545-100, Fort Drive, Fort Drive #1, William W.Harts, Col, U.S. Army, Officer in Charge, to General William M. Black, Chief of Engineers, June 17, 1917.

[2] Record Group 42, Records of the Office of Public Buildings and Grounds, National Archives (hereafter referred to as RG42), Office of Public Buildings and Grounds, General Correspondence, 307, Public Grounds: Extension of Park System, Civil War Forts Parkway, October 1919 listing of forts RG77; Entry 103, Correspondence, 1894-1923, #124636.

[3] RG42, Office of Public Buildings and Grounds, General Correspondence, 307, Public Grounds: Extension of Park System, Civil War Forts Parkway, including 307/6-7, Board of Commissioners of the District of Columbia to Honorable Lawrence Y. Sherman, Chairman, Committee on the District of Columbia, United States Senate, November 8, 1919; Washington, D.C. Archives, D.C. Records, Central Classified Files: Engineer Department (ED), Engineer Department Case Files, 1897-1955, #155186-3, HR 10695, 60th Congress, 1st Session, November 19, 1919; *Journal of the House of Representatives of the United States . . .* 66th Congress, 1st Session (Washington, DC: The Government Printing Office, 1919), 594 (HR 10695).

[4] RG42, Office of Public Buildings and Grounds, General Correspondence, 307, Public Grounds: Extension of Park System, Civil War Forts Parkway, October 1919 listing of forts; Record Group 46, Records of the United States Senate, National Archives (hereafter referred to as RG46), 67th Congress, Papers Relating to specific Bills and Resolutions, S.1-50, Box 1, Letter from Cuno H. Rudolph, President, Commissioners of the District of Columbia, to Honorable L. Heisler Ball, Chairman, Committee on the District of Columbia, United States Senate, April 11, 1921, submitted with a proposed bill; Washington, D.C. Archives, D.C. Records, Central Classified Files: Engineer Department (ED), Engineer Department Case Files, 1897-1955, #155186-1, Cuno H. Rudolph, President, Commissioners of the District of Columbia, to Honorable Benjamin Focht, Chairman, Committee on the District of Columbia, House of Representatives, April 11, 1921; Washington, D.C. Archives, D.C. Records, Central Classified Files: Engineer Department (ED), Engineer Department Case Files, 1897-1955, #155186-3, HR 10695, 60th Congress, 1st Session, November 19, 1919; RG77, Entry 103, Correspondence, 1894-1923, #124636; RG42, Office of Public Buildings and Public Parks, General Correspondence, 307, Public Grounds: Extension of Park System: Civil War Forts Parkway; *Journal of the House of Representatives of the United States . . .* 66th Congress, 1st Session (Washington, DC: The Government Printing Office, 1919), 594 (HR 10695).

[5] *Journal of the Senate of the United States . . .* 67th Congress, 1st Session (Washington, DC: The Government Printing Office, 1922), 14 (S4); *Journal of the House of Representatives of the United States . . .* 67th Congress, 1st Session (Washington, DC: The Government Printing Office, 1921), 497 (HR 8792); *Journal of the House of Representatives of the United States . . .* 67th Congress, 2d Session, 19221-22 (Washington, DC: The Government Printing Office, 1922), 116 (HR 8792); *Journal of the Senate of the United States . . .* 68th Congress, 1st Session, 1923-24

(Washington, DC: The Government Printing Office, 1924), 58 (S1340); *Journal of the Senate of the United States*. 68th Congress, 2d Session, 1924-25 (Washington, DC: The Government Printing Office, 1925), 50 (S1340); "Parkway to Connect Forts in District of Columbia," *House Report No. 649*, 67th Congress, 2d Session, February 3, 1923; "Parkway Connecting Civil War Forts," Calendar No. 627, *Senate Report No. 585*, 68th Congress, 1st Session, May 20, 1924, May 20 (calendar day, May 22), 1924; RG46, 67th Congress, Papers relating to specific Bills and Resolutions, S.1-50, Box 1; Washington, D.C. Archives, D.C. Records, Central Classified Files: Engineer Department (ED), Engineer Department Case Files, 1897-1955, #155186-3; "Linking of Forts Embodied in Plan," *The Evening Star*, December 4, 1925; RG328, General Records, Planning Files, 1924-67, 545-100, Fort Drive, Fort Drive #1, S1340, 68th Congress, 2D Session, January 2, 1925; Record Group 66, Records of the Commission on Fine Arts, National Archives (hereafter referred to as RG66), Entry 17, Project Files, 1910-52, Forts, Fort Lincoln Cemetery, Prince Georges County, MD; Memorandum, May 14, 1921, "FORT DRIVE AND EASTERN AVENUE.

[6] William Bushong. *Historic Resource Study: Rock Creek Park - District of Columbia*. Washington, DC: The Government Printing Office, 1990, 934-95, 102; RG42, Office of Public Buildings and Grounds, General Correspondence, 307, Public Grounds: Extension of Park System, Civil War Forts Parkway, 307/8 , Judge C.D. Bundy, Board of Trade, District of Columbia, to Office of Public Buildings and Grounds, received on January 10, 1920 ; RG328, General Records, Planning Files, 1924-67, 545-100, Fort Drive, #2, T.C. Jeffers, Landscape Architect,"THE FORT DRIVE, A Chronological History of the More Important Actions and Events Relating Thereto," Feb. 7, 1947; T.C. Jeffers, "A Brief History of THE FORT DRIVE — Evolution of its Concept and Function," March 17, 1947; and T.S. Settle, "Legal Authority for Acquisition of Land and Construction of the Fort to Fort Drive, in the District of Columbia," November 14-15, 1940.

[7] William Bushong. *Historic Resource Study: Rock Creek Park - District of Columbia*. Washington, DC: The Government Printing Office, 1990, 93-95, 102; RG328, General Records, Planning Files, 1924-67, 545-100, Fort Drive, #2, T.C. Jeffers, Landscape Architect,"THE FORT DRIVE, A Chronological History of the More Important Actions and Events Relating Thereto," Feb. 7, 1947; T.C. Jeffers, "A Brief History of THE FORT DRIVE — Evolution of its Concept and Function," March 17, 1947; and T.S. Settle, "Legal Authority for Acquisition of Land and Construction of the Fort to Fort Drive, in the District of Columbia," November 14-15, 1940.

[8] Walton, Thomas. "The 1901 McMillan Commission: Beaux Arts Plan for the Nation's Capital." Ph.D. dissertation, Catholic University, 1980. 128, 149; William Bushong, *Historic Resource Study: Rock Creek Park - District of Columbia* (Washington, DC: The Government Printing Office, 1990), 93-95, 102; RG328, General Records, Planning Files, 1924-67, 545-100, Fort Drive, #2, T.C. Jeffers, Landscape Architect,"THE FORT DRIVE, A Chronological History of the More Important Actions and Events Relating Thereto,' 'February 7, 1947; T.C. Jeffers, "A Brief History of THE FORT DRIVE — Evolution of its Concept and Function", March 17, 1947; and T.S. Settle, "Legal Authority for Acquisition of Land and Construction of the Fort to Fort Drive, in the District of Columbia," November 14-15, 1940.

[9] For important text of the Capper-Cramton Act see Appendix B; Walton, Thomas. "The 1901 McMillan Commission: Beaux Arts Plan for the Nation's Capital." Ph.D. dissertation, Catholic University, 1980. 128, 149; William Bushong, *Historic Resource Study: Rock Creek Park - District of Columbia* (Washington, DC: The Government Printing Office, 1990), 93-95, 102; RG328, General Records, Planning Files, 1924-67, 545-100, Fort Drive, #2, T.C. Jeffers, Landscape Architect,"THE FORT DRIVE, A Chronological History of the More Important Actions and Events Relating Thereto," February 7, 1947; T.C. Jeffers, "A Brief History of THE FORT DRIVE — Evolution of its

Concept and Function," March 17, 1947; and T.S. Settle, "Legal Authority for Acquisition of Land and Construction of the Fort to Fort Drive, in the District of Columbia," November 14-15, 1940; *Statutes at Large*, Volume 46, page 482, Public Law No. 284, 71st Congress, approved May 29, 1930.

[10] "National Capital Park and Planning Commission." In H.S. Wagner and Charles G. Sauers, *Study of the Organization of the National Capital Parks* (Washington, DC: The National Park Service, National Capital Parks, 1939), 40.

[11] RG328, General Records, Planning Files, 1924-67, 545-100, Fort Drive, #2; T.C. Jeffers, "THE FORT DRIVE, A Chronological History of the More Important Actions and Events Relating Thereto," February 7, 1947; T.C. Jeffers, "A Brief History of THE FORT DRIVE — Evolution of its Concept and Function," March 17, 1947; Civil War Round Table of the District of Columbia, "Washington Needs The Fort Memorial Freeway,"Pamphlet, (1953?).

[12] RG328, General Records, Planning Files, 1924-67, 545-100 Fort Drive, Fort Drive #1, J.E. Wood to Lt. Col. C.O. Sherrill, March 10, 1924, J.C. Langdon to Major Brown July 31 and August 3, 1925, U.S. Grant, III, to Mr. D.W. O'Donohue, Union Trust Building, July 31, 1926, "Fort Drive"by C.W. Eliot, City Planner, and C.W. Eliot to Major Brown May 10, 1929; Fort Drive, #2, T.C. Jeffers, Landscape Architect,"THE FORT DRIVE, a Chronological History of the More Important Actions and Events Relating Thereto," February 7, 1947; Chris Shaheen, "The Fort Drive: The Influence and Adaption of a 20th Century Planning Effort in Washington, D.C. Paper in George Washington University Historic Preservation Course (Professor Richard Longstreth), May 30, 1994, 4.

[13] RG328, General Records,Planning Files, 1924-67, 545-100 Fort Drive, Fort Drive #1,T.C. Jeffers to Captain Chisolm, March 13, 1931 and "Emergency Public Works Program Brief Justification For Fort Drive Projects," August 31, 1933; and Fort Drive, #2; Fort Drive, Acquisition of Land, February 1, 1947, and T.C.Jeffers, "THE FORT DRIVE, A Chronological History of the More Important Actions and Events Relating Thereto," February 7, 1947; T.C. Jeffers, "A Brief History of THE FORT DRIVE — Evolution of its Concept and Function," March 17, 1947; Civil War Round Table of the District of Columbia, "Washington Needs The Fort Memorial Freeway,"Pamphlet, (1953?).

[14] Record Group 79, Records of the National Park Service, National Archives (hereafter referred to as RG79), Records of the Branch of Recreation, Land Protection, and State Cooperation,
Narratuive Reports Concerning ECW (CCC) Projects in NPS Areas, 1933-35, District of Columbia, Box 12, Narrative Report, NP Camp #7, Benning, D.C., April 1-September 30, 1935; Box 13, Camp NP-7, Narrative Report, April -October 1935, Camp Name, Fort Dupont, projects 7-10—7-22; NP Camp 7, Benning, D.C., Narrative Report, October 1934-April 1935; NP Camp 7, Narrative Report, October 1934-January 1935; RG328, General Records, Planning Files, 1924-67, 545-100, Fort Drive, Fort Drive #1, T.S. Settle, Secretary, Memorandum to Mr. Gillen, March 5, 1940, SUBJ: Fort Drive; U.S., Office of National Capital Parks, "A History of National Capital Parks," By Cornelius W. Heine (Washington, DC: National Capital Parks, National Park Service, 1953), 31; Christine Sadler, "One More Mile and the District Will Have a Driveway Linking Forts, Road to Pass Fortifications of Civil War, Will Run Along Rims of Hills That Make Saucer of City, Expected to Be One of Nation's Most Scenic and Historic, *The Washington Post*, Sunday, October 10, 1937.

[15] Washington, D.C. Archives. D.C. Records, Central Classified Files: Engineer Department (ED). Engineer Department Case Files, 1897-1955, #248515, including completed PWA application; RG328, General Records,Planning Files, 1924-67, 545-100 Fort Drive, Fort Drive, #2 T.C. Jeffers, "THE FORT DRIVE, A Chronological History of the

More Important Actions and Events Relating Thereto," February 7, 1947; and T.C. Jeffers, "A Brief History of THE FORT DRIVE — Evolution of its Concept and Function," March 17, 1947; Civil War Round Table of the District of Columbia, "Washington Needs The Fort Memorial Freeway,"Pamphlet, (1953?).

16 RG328, General Records,Planning Files, 1924-67, 545-100 Fort Drive, Fort Drive, #2 T.C. Jeffers, "THE FORT DRIVE, A Chronological History of the More Important Actions and Events Relating Thereto," February 7, 1947; and T.C. Jeffers, "A Brief History of THE FORT DRIVE — Evolution of its Concept and Function," March 17, 1947; Civil War Round Table of the District of Columbia, "Washington Needs The Fort Memorial Freeway,"Pamphlet, (1953?); Gerald G. Gross, "Planning Board Seeks Funds for Fort Drive," *The Washington Post*, November. 15, 1940; "History of Fort Drive," In National Capital Planning Commission, *Fort Park System: A Re-evaluation Study of Fort Drive, Washington, D.C.* April 1965 By Fred W. Tuemmler and Associates, College Park, Maryland (Washington, DC: National Capital Planning Commission, 1965), 3; Shaheen, "Fort Drive," 9-10.

17 RG328, General Records,Planning Files, 1924-67, 545-100 Fort Drive, Fort Drive, #2 T.C. Jeffers, "THE FORT DRIVE, A Chronological History of the More Important Actions and Events Relating Thereto," February 7, 1947; and T.C. Jeffers, "A Brief History of THE FORT DRIVE — Evolution of its Concept and Function," March 17, 1947; Civil War Round Table of the District of Columbia, "Washington Needs The Fort Memorial Freeway,"Pamphlet, (1953?); Christine Sadler, "One More Mile and the District Will Have a Driveway Linking Forts, Road to Pass Fortifications of Civil War, Will Run Along Rims of Hills That Make Saucer of City, Expected to Be One of Nation's Most Scenic and Historic, *The Washington Post*, Sunday, October 10, 1937; Thomas Walton, "The 1901 McMillan Commission: Beaux Arts Plan for the Nation's Capital," Ph.D. dissertation, Catholic University, 1980, 149; "Fort Drive," *The Evening Star*, Saturday, November 16, 1940; Gerald G. Gross, "Planning Board Seeks Funds for Fort Drive," *The Washington Post*, November. 15, 1940; "History of Fort Drive," In National Capital Planning Commission, *Fort Park System: A Re-evaluation Study of Fort Drive, Washington, D.C.* April 1965 By Fred W. Tuemmler and Associates, College Park, Maryland (Washington, DC: National Capital Planning Commission, 1965), 3; Civil War Round Table of the District of Columbia, "Washington Needs The Fort Memorial Freeway," Pamphlet, (1953?) Gerald G. Gross, "Planning Board Seeks Funds for Fort Drive," *The Washington Post*, November. 15, 1940.

18 *An Illustrated History: The City of Washington*, By the Junior League of Washington, Edited by Thomas Froncek (New York: Alfred A. Knopf, 1979), 320; RG328, NCPC, General Records, Planning files, 1924-67, 535, Parks & Recreation, Battery Kemble Park, John Nolen, Jr., Director of Planning to Mr. T.P. Pendleton, Chief Topographical. Engineer, Geologic Survey, Department of the Interior, Washington, December 29, 1944, Subj.: Name of Battery Kemble Park; RG328, General Records, Planning Files, 1924-67, 535, Parks and Reservations, Fort Dupont Park, John Nolen, Jr., Director of Planning, Memorandum to Mr. Wirth, SUBJ: Fort Dupont Park, June 5, 1937; " Fort Dupont Park Suits Under Way,"*The Evening Star*, December 11, 1935; Rock Creek Park Files, Battery Kemble, Office of Public Buildings and Public Parks of the National Capital, January 27, 1931, General Order No. 384, Subject: Acquisition of Land; "Fort Foote Military Reservation in Prince Georges County, MD; "Calendar No. 1101, *Senate Report No. 1036*, 68th Congress, 2d Session, February 3, 1925; U.S., Army Corps of Engineers, Washington District, *A Historical Summary of the Works of the Corps of Engineers in Washington, DC and Vicinity 1852-1952* By Sacket L. Duryee (Washington, DC: U.S., U.S. Army Corps of Engineers, Washington District, 1952), 25; Ed Fitzgerald to Rock Comstock, September 24, 1973, CRBIB Material, Fort Circle Parks, in Stephen Potter's Office, National Park Service, National Capital Parks; "Fort Foote, "*The Evening Star*, June 1, 1926; "Fort Foote Wanted in D. C. Park System," *Evening Star*, April 29, 1924; RG46, 69th Congress, Papers relating to specific Bills and Resolutions, E-1, Box 39, Dwight Davis, Secretary of War to Honorable James W. Wadsworth, Jr., Chairman, Com-

mittee on Military Affairs, United States Senate, August 19, 1925; "Fort Foote Ordered Delayed," *The Evening Star*, June 12, 1926; National Park Service, National Capital Region, Binder titled Fort Foote, in Gary Scott's Office, Office of Public Buildings and Public Parks of the National Capital, General Order No. 432, November 6, 1931, issued by U.S. Grant, III, SUBJ: Acquisition of Land by Transfer, "1; Martha Strayer, "Old Fort Foote, a Forlorn and Forgotten Place," *The Washington Daily News*, Monday, July 20, 1931; *Journal of the House of Representatives of the United States . . .* 68th Congress, 2d Session, 1924-25 (Washington, DC: The Government Printing Office, 1924), 280, 288, 476 (S.J.117); *Journal of the House of Representatives of the United States . . .* 69th Congress, 1st session 1925-26 (Washington, DC: The Government Printing Office, 1926), 739, 1099 (HR 12644); *Journal of the Senate of the United States . . .* 69th Congress, 1st Session (Washington, DC: The Government Printing Office, 1926), 436, 712 (S4401); *Journal of the Senate of the United States . . .* 68th , 1st Session, 1923-24 (Washington, DC: The Government Printing Office, 1924), 304, 578 (SJ117); *Journal of the Senate of the United States . . .* 68th Congress, 2d Session, 1924-25 (Washington, DC: The Government Printing Office, 1925), 157, 204 (SJ117) [February 17, 1925, approved public resolution No. 46]; Journal of the House of Representatives of the United States . . . 68th Congress, 2d Session, 1924-25 (Washington, DC: The Government Printing Office, 1924), 95, 290, 444 (HR11365); *Journal of the House of Representatives of the United States . . .* 70th Congress, 1st Session, 1927-28 (Washington, DC: The Government Printing Office, 1928), 378, 11744 (HR10556); *Journal of the House of Representatives of the United States . . .* 71st Congress, 2d session, 1929-30 (Washington, DC: The Government Printing Office, 1930), 431, 523 (HR11489); "National Military Park to Commemorate Battle of Fort Stevens," Hearings Before the Committee on Military Affairs, House of Representatives, Sixty-Eighth Congress, Second Session, on H.R. 11365, Monday, January 12, 1925, Statement of Hon. Samuel E. Cook of Indiana. (Washington, DC: The Government Printing Office, 1925); Union Calendar No. 520, H.R. 11365, [*House Report No. 1537*], 68th Congress, 2D Session, February 20, 1925; "Commemoration of Certain Military Historic Events, and for Other Purposes," *House Report No. 1525*, 71st Congress, 2d Session, May 19, 1930, 24; RG42, Entry 109, Newspaper Clippings, 1926-27, Box 5, "Land Approved For Parks," newspaper article, 1926; Mark Tooley, "Battle at Fort Stevens Saved,"*The Washington Post*, August 6, 1994; Record Group 233, Records of the United States House of Representatives, National Archives (hereafter referred to as RG233), Papers Accompanying Specific Bills and Resolutions, HR70A-D20, Box 375—H.R. 10556, 70th Congress, 1st Session, In the House of Representatives, February 6, 1928; Bruce L. Brager, "Fort Stevens--Lincoln Under Fire." *Northern Virginian*, 12, July-August 1982, 22; "Ft. Stevens Falls in Building Drive," *The Evening Star*, May 16, 1925; "Historic Spot Is Site For New Homes," *Washington Times*, Oct 29, 1927; William J. Wheatley, "Fort De Russy to be Restored: Surrounding Section in Rock Creek Park Being Cleared to Open Area," *The Evening Star*, Dec. 5, 1926; "Fort Bayard Park Has Much History," *The Washington Post*, July 13, 1930; Judith Beck Helm, *Tenleytown, D.C. Country Village into A City Neighborhood* (Washington, DC: Tennally Press, 1981), 363.

[19] RG79, Records of the Branch of Recreation, Land Protection, and State Cooperation, Narrative Reports Concerning ECW (CCC) Projects in NPS Areas, 1933-35, District of Columbia, Boxes 11, National Capital Parks, Narrative Report covering Fifth Enrollment Period, ECW Camp N.A. #1, Washington, DC, Apr-Oct 1935; Reservation #412, Reservation #443, and Reservation #475, Box 12, Narrative Report, NP Camp #7, Benning, DC, April 1—September 30, 1935, Box 13, Camp NP-7, Narrative Report, April-October 1935, Camp Name—Fort Dupont—Project 7-1—7-9, and projects 7-10—7-22, NP-7, Benning, DC, General Report for Second Enrollment Period, Oct 1933-Apr. 1934, Field Work at Fort Dupont, NP Camp 7, Benning, DC, Narrative Report, Oct 1934-April 1935, minor road construction at Fort Dupont, cleanup at Reservation 544, Ft. Totten, NP Camp 7, Narrative Report, Oct 1934-Jan 1935, work on Fort Drive, NP Camp 7, Benning, DC, Narrative Report, July-Oct 1934, sewer at Fort Dupont, Ft. Foote, General Cleanup; RG328, General Records, Planning Files, 1924-67, 545-100, Fort Drive, Fort Drive #1, T.S. Settle, Secretary, Memorandum to Mr. Gillen, March 5, 1940, SUBJ: Fort Drive; U.S., Office of National Capital Parks, "A

History of National Capital Parks," By Cornelius W. Heine (Washington, DC: National Capital Parks, National Park Service, 1953), 31; Christine Sadler, "One More Mile and the District Will Have a Driveway Linking Forts, Road to Pass Fortifications of Civil War, Will Run Along Rims of Hills That Make Saucer of City, Expected to Be One of Nation's Most Scenic and Historic, *The Washington Post*, Sunday, October 10, 1937; RG328, General Records, Planning Files, 1924-67, 545-100, Fort Drive, Fort Drive #1, T.S. Settle, Secretary, Memorandum to Mr. Gillen, March 5, 1940, SUBJ: Fort Drive; The Rambler (Richard Rogers), "Old Fort Resists Siege of Time," *The Evening Star*, Oct. 19, 1956; Benjamin Franklin Cooling, III and Walton H. Owen, II, *Mr. Lincoln's Forts: A Guide to the Civil War Defenses of Washington* (Shippensburg, PA: White Mane Publishing Company, 1988), 161; Bernard Kohn, "Restored Civil War Fort Is New Sightseeing Shrine," *The Sunday Star*, July 4, 1937.

[20] Martha Strayer, "Old Fort Foote, A Forlorn and Forgotten Place," *The Washington Daily News*, Monday, July 20, 1931; RG66, Entry 17, Project Files, 1910-52, Forts, Fort Stanton; RG328, General Records, Planning Files, 1924-67, 535, Parks and Reservations, Fort Totten Park, Extract from minutes of the 55th meeting of the National Capital Parks and Planning Commission held on March 6, 1938 and Extract from minutes of the 122nd meeting of the National Capital Parks and Planning Commission held on October 28 & 29, 1937; "Park Board May Wreck Historic Fort," *The Washington Post*, October 28, 1937; RG66, Entry 17, Project Files, 1910-52, Forts, Fort Dupont—Water Tower; *Statutes at Large*, 67th Congress, 1921-23, Vol. 42, Pt. 1 (Washington, D.C.: The Government Printing Office 1923), 1368; "Bunker Mentality," *City Paper*, January 13-19, 1995; Judith Beck Helm, *Tenleytown, D. C.: Country Village into City Neighborhood* (Washington, DC: Tennally Press, 1981), 470; RG328, General Records, Planning Files, 1924-67, 535, Parks and Reservations, Fort Foote, Extract from minutes of 156th meeting of National Capital Parks and Planning Commission held on Dec. 19-20, 1930 or 40?; RG66, Entry 17, Project Files, 1910-52, Forts, Fort Reno—Water Tower, "New Fourth-High Tower at Reno, Built in 1928.

[21] RG328, General Records, Planning Files, 1924-67, 545-100, Fort Drive, Fort Drive #2, Committee on—A.E. Demaray, Associate Director, National Park Service, Memorandum for Secretary, August 12, 1944, and T.C. Jeffers, Landscape Architect, "THE FORT DRIVE, A Chronological History of the More Important Actions and Events Relating Thereto," February 7, 1947; RG66, Entry 17, Project Files, 1910-52, Fort Drive, John Russell Young, President, Board of Commissioners, District of Columbia to Hon. Gilmore D. Clarke, Chairman, The Commission of Fine Arts, Interior Department Building, April 4, 1947; Civil War Round Table of the District of Columbia, "Washington Needs The Fort Memorial Freeway," Pamphlet (1953?); Thomas Walton, "The 1901 McMillan Commission: Beaux Arts Plan for the Nation's Capital," Ph.D. dissertation, Catholic University, 1980, 149; Cooperative Agreements and Historic Site Designation Orders, Agreement with District of Columbia, Memorandum of Agreement of October 24, 1944 Between the National Park Service and the District of Columbia Relating to Development of Two Sections of Fort Drive.

[22] RG328, General Records, Planning files, 1924-67, 545-100, Fort Drive, Committee on—A.E. Demaray, Associate Director, National Park Service, Memorandum for Secretary, August 12, 1944; Civil War Round Table of the District of Columbia, "Washington Needs The Fort Memorial Freeway," Pamphlet (1953?); Thomas Walton, "The 1901 McMillan Commission: Beaux Arts Plan for the Nation's Capital," Ph.D. dissertation, Catholic University, 1980, 149; RG66, Entry 17, Project Files, 1910-52, Fort Drive, John Russell Young, President, Board of Commissioners, District of Columbia to Hon. Gilmore D. Clarke, Chairman, The Commission of Fine Arts, Interior Department Building, April 4, 1947, and Budget Officer and Assessor, District of Columbia, to the Commissioners, District of Colimbia, Subject: Acquisition of Land, January 21, 1947; RG328, General Records, Planning Files, 1924-67, 545-100, Fort Drive, Fort Drive #1, T.S. Settle, Secretary, Memorandum to Mr. Gillen, March 5, 1940, SUBJ: Fort

Drive; Civil War Round Table of the District of Columbia, "Washington Needs The Fort Memorial Freeway," Pamphlet (1953?); Gerald G. Gross, "Planning Board Seeks Funds for Fort Drive," *The Washington Post*, November 15, 1940; Helm, *Tenleytown*, 448; "Park Board Approves Changes In Fort Drive Project Plans." *The Washington Post*, June 21, 1947; "Fort Drive Up for Study Today." *The Washington Post*, March 20, 1947; "Fowler to Stick To His Figures on Fort Drive Cost." *The Washington Post*, February 25, 1947.

[23] "History of Fort Drive," In National Capital Planning Commission, *Fort Park System: A Re-evaluation Study of Fort Drive, Washington, D.C.* April 1965 By Fred W. Tuemmler and Associates, College Park, Maryland (Washington, DC: National Capital Planning Commission, 1965), 3-9; Civil War Round Table of the District of Columbia, "Washington Needs The Fort Memorial Freeway," Pamphlet (1953?); "District, Park Service Clash Over Highway vs. Parkway." *The Washington Post*, April 2, 1961;Willard Clopton, "Park Service Weighs Future of Fort Drive," *The Washington Post*, Monday, April 30, 1962; Martha Strayer, "JFK Settles Battle Over Ft. Drive," *Washington Daily News*, May 28, 1963.

[24] "A Ring of Parks," *The Washington Post*, May 14, 1965; "Beauty Duty Sought for 16 Old Forts, *The Washington Post*, May 7, 1965; Henry Aubin, "District's Old Forts: Squirrels Man Ivied Ramparts," *The Washington Post*, Monday, December 28, 1970; National Capital Planning Commission, *Fort Park System*, iv.

[25] Willard Clopton, "Park Service Weighs Future of Fort Drive," *The Washington Post*, Monday, April 30, 1962; "Fort Drive," *The Evening Star*, Saturday, November 16, 1940; Gerald G. Gross, "Planning Board Seeks Funds for Fort Drive," *The Washington Post*, November. 15, 1940; U.S., Office of National Capital Parks, "A History of National Capital Parks,"By Cornelius W. Heine (Washington, DC: National Capital Parks, National Park Service, 1953), 88; Civil War Round Table of the District of Columbia, "Washington Needs The Fort Memorial Freeway," Pamphlet (1953?); Judith Beck Helm, *Tenleytown, D.C. Country Village into A City Neighborhood* (Washington, DC: Tennally Press, 1981), 484; National Capital Planning Commission. *Fort Park System: A Re-evaluation Study of Fort Drive, Washington, D.C.* April 1965, By Fred W. Tuemmler and Associates, College Park, Maryland (Washington, DC: National Capital Planning Commission, 1965), 1, 8.

[26] National Capital Planning Commission. *Fort Park System: A Re-evaluation Study of Fort Drive, Washington, D.C.* April 1965, By Fred W. Tuemmler and Associates, College Park, Maryland (Washington, DC: National Capital Planning Commission, 1965), 1, 8.

[27] U.S., National Capital Planning Commission, *Worthy of the Nation: The History of Planning for the National Capital* Frederick Gutheim, Consultant (Washington, DC: Smithsonian Institution Press, 1977), 194; Washington, D.C. Archives, D.C. Records, Central Classified Files: Engineer Department (ED), Engineer Department Case Files, 1897-1955, #155186-3, HR 10695, 60th Congress, 1st Session, November 19, 1919; RG328, General Records, Planning files, 1924-67, 545-100, Fort Drive, Committee on, A.E. Demaray, Associate Director, National Park Service, Memorandum for Secretary, August 12, 1944; RG66, Entry 17, Project Files, 1910-52, Fort Drive, Gilmore D. Clarke, Chairman, Commission on Fine Arts, to Honorable John Russell Young, President, Board of Commissioners, District of Columbia, March 6, 1947.

[28] RG328, General Records, Planning Files, 1924-67, 545-100, Fort Drive, Fort Drive #1, Carey H. Brown, Engineer, to The Newspaper Information Service, 1322 New York Avenue, Washington, DC, May 4, 1927, 6; U.S., National Capital Planning Commission, *Worthy of the Nation: The History of Planning for the National Capital*

Frederick Gutheim, Consultant (Washington, DC: Smithsonian Institution Press, 1977), 196; "Fort Sites Eyed for Future Use," *The Washington Post*, Friday, October 2, 1964.

29 USACE\CEMVS\ED-U.S. Corps of Engineers, St. Louis District, Report on Fort Reno, AAA Site Fort Reno - Washington, D.C., Project Number -CO3DCO48401, March 1997, 4.0 SITE HISTORY, 4.1 HISTORICAL SITE SUMMARY, 4.1.1 General Site History; RG338, Unit Records, Anti-Aircraft Artillery Brigade, Box 20, History of the 36th AAA Battalion," not dated c. 1954, 3; Helm, *Tenleytown*, 534-35; Neighborhood Planning Councils 2 and 3, *Footsteps: Historical Walking Tours of Chevy Chase, Cleveland Park, Tenleytown , Friendship* (Washington, DC: Neighborhood Planning Councils 2 and 3, 1976), 10.

30 "Huge Reservoir Is Taking Shape," *The Washington Post and Times Herald*, Thursday, May 10, 1956; "Bunker Mentality," *City Paper*, January 13-19, 1995; Judith Beck Helm; *Tenleytown, D.C. Country Village into A City Neighborhood* (Washington, DC: Tennally Press, 1981), 535; RG66, Entry 17, Project Files, 1910-52, Forts, Fort Reno—Water tower; John M. Johnson, Colonel, Corps of Engineers, District Engineer, to Commission of Fine Arts, November 1, 1944.

31 Cooling, *Mr. Lincoln's Forts*, 232; *House Executive Document No. 361*, 81st Congress, 1st Session, "Supplemental Estimate of Appropriation for the Department of the Interior," October 11, 1949; RG328, General Records, Planning Files, 1924-67, 535, Parks and Reservations, Fort Totten Park, Irving C. Root, Superintendent, National Park Service, National Capital Parks, to Mr. Edmund H. Brook, National Brick and Supply Co January 15, 1948; RG328, General Records, Planning Files, 1924-67, 535, Parks and Reservations, Fort Totten Park, Extract from minutes of the 190th meeting of the National Capital Park and Planning Commission held on Dec. 16, 1943; RG328, General Records, Planning Files, 1924-67, 535, Parks and Reservations, Fort Totten Park, Letter of February 14, 1947; RG328, General Records, Planning Files, 1924-67, 535, Parks and Reservations, Fort Dupont Park; A.E. Demaray, Acting Executive Director, to Lt. Col. William C. Ready, Corps of Engineers, Mid-Atlantic Division, Dec. 2, 1944.

32 Martha Strayer, "Old Fort Foote, a Forlorn and Forgotten Place," *The Washington Daily News*, Monday, July 20, 1931; Louise Daniel Hutchinson, *The Anacostia Story: 1608-1930* (Washington, DC: Published for the Anacostia Neighborhood Museum of the Smithsonian Institution by the Smithsonian Institution Press, 1977), 126, 129, 135; Mark Tooley, "Battle at Fort Stevens Saved." *The Washington Post*, August 6, 1994.

33 Reed Hansen, "Civil War to Civil Concern: A History of Fort Marcy, Virginia,"Masters thesis in History, George Mason University, 1973, 71, 74-77, 80, 83, 88; Eleanor Lee Templeman, " Fairfax Heritage No. 3: Fort Marcy's Fate Uncertain, *Northern Virginia Sun*, February 28, 1958; "Fort Marcey's Guns Protected Bridge Entering 'Georgetown Pike," *Fairfax Herald*, February 25, 1972, 7; "Civil War's Fort Marcy Slated to Become Park," *The Washington Post and Times Herald*, Thursday, March 13, 1958; Jack Eisen, "Unreconstructed Rebels Will Not Buy Civil War Fort Marcy for Parkway," *The Washington Post*, April 3, 1958; Jean M. White, "Access Road Will Be Built to Fort Marcy," *The Washington Post*, November 6, 1960; "Fairfax Official Recalls how "Sit-In" Saved Historic Fort From Bulldozers," *The Washington Post*, July 30, 1963; "Housewife's Defiance Saved Fort Marcy," *The Evening Star*, July 29, 1963; RG328, General Records, Planning Files, 1924-67, 543-36, Civil War Forts, Preservation of, Harry T. Thompson, Acting Superintendent, National Capital Parks, Memorandum to Director, National Capital Planning commission, SUBJ: Preservation of the Civil War Forts, May 28, 1954, and Stanley McClure, Assistant Chief, National Memorials and Historic Sites Section, National Capital Parks, NPS, to Messers. Kelly, Thompson, Gartside, Jett and Sager, May 24, 1954, SUBJ: Preservation of the Civil War Forts, 1952-54; U.S., Department of the Interior, National Park Service, George Washington Memorial Parkway, *Earthworks Landscape Management Plan. Fort*

Marcy. (Washington, DC: U.S., Department of the Interior, National Park Service, George Washington Memorial Parkway, 1995).

[34] RG328, General Records, Planning Files, 1924-67, 543-36, Civil War Forts, Preservation of, Stanley McClure, Assistant Chief, National Memorials and Historic Sites Section, National Capital Parks, National Park Service, to Messers. Kelly, Thompson, Gartside, Jett and Sager, May 24, 1954, SUBJ: Preservation of the Civil War Forts, 1952-54.

[35] "Site of 7 Corners Center Once Called Fort Buffalo," *The Washington Post*, Oct. 3, 1956; "Modern Shopping Center Stands Near Civil War Shooting Grounds, *The Washington Daily News*, October 3, 1956; "Fairfax Official Recalls how "sit-In" Saved Historic Fort From Bulldozers," *The Washington Post*, July 30, 1963; "County Seeks to Preserve Ft. Reynolds," *The Washington Post*, September 9, 1954; "Gun Battery Yields Only Yankee Button, *The Evening Star*, April 25, 1958; "Old Gun Emplacement Halts School Bulldozer, " *The Evening Star*, April 23, 1958; Jack Eisen, "Unreconstructed Rebels Will Not Buy Civil War Fort Marcy for Parkway," *The Washington Post*, April 3, 1958; Jerry Kline, "Alexandria Restores Old Civil War Fort," Star, Aug 5, 1962; "Alexandria to Rebuild Civil War Fort Ward," *The Washington Post*, September 1, 1960; Deborah Churdhman, Searching for the Civil War [Report from the Forts]. *The Washington Post, Weekend*, October 23, 1981, 1, 10; Jim Ryan, "History Afoot At the Forts." *The Washington Post, Weekend*, January 6, 1989; Anne H. Oman, "The Forts of Washington: Only Two Saw Hostile Action." *The Washington Post, Weekend*, May 27, 1983, 58; Eugene L. Meyer, "Holding Down the Fort in D.C.," *The Washington Post*, Friday, January 23, 1987.

[36] RG328, General Records, Planning Files, 1924-67, 543-36, Civil War Forts, Preservation of, Stanley McClure, Assistant Chief, National Memorials and Historic Sites Section, National Capital Parks, National Park Service, to Messers. Kelly, Thompson, Gartside, Jett and Sager, May 24, 1954, SUBJ: Preservation of the Civil War Forts, 1952-54; Roy C. Brewer, "Fort Scott—Past, Present, and Future," *The Arlington Historical Magazine*, 3 (October 1965), 46; "County Seeks to Preserve Ft. Reynolds," *The Washington Post*, September 9, 1954; "Site of 7 Corners Center Once Called Fort Buffalo," *The Washington Post*, October 3, 1956; "Modern Shopping Center Stands Near Civil War Shooting Grounds, *The Washington Daily News*, October 3, 1956; "Fairfax Official Recalls how 'Sit-In' Saved Historic Fort From Bulldozers, *The Washington Post*, July 30, 1963; "County Seeks to Preserve Ft. Reynolds," *The Washington Post*, September 9, 1954; "Gun Battery Yields Only Yankee Button, *The Evening Star*, April 25, 1958; "Old Gun Emplacement Halts School Bulldozer, " *The Evening Star*, April 23, 1958; Jack Eisen, "Unreconstructed Rebels Will Not Buy Civil War Fort Marcy for Parkway," *The Washington Post*, April 3, 1958; Jerry Kline, "Alexandria Restores Old Civil War Fort," Star, Aug 5, 1962; "Alexandria to Rebuild Civil War Fort Ward," *The Washington Post*, September 1, 1960; Deborah Churdhman, Searching for the Civil War [Report from the Forts]. *The Washington Post, Weekend*, October 23, 1981, 1, 10; Jim Ryan, "History Afoot At the Forts." *The Washington Post, Weekend*, January 6, 1989; Anne H. Oman, "The Forts of Washington: Only Two Saw Hostile Action." *The Washington Post, Weekend*, May 27, 1983, 58; Eugene L. Meyer, "Holding Down the Fort in D.C.," *The Washington Post*, Friday, January 23, 1987.

[37] RG328, General Records, Planning Files, 1924-67, 543-36, Civil War Forts, Preservation of, Stanley McClure, Assistant Chief, National Memorials and Historic Sites Section, National Capital Parks, National Park Service, to Messers. Kelly, Thompson, Gartside, Jett and Sager, May 24, 1954, SUBJ: Preservation of the Civil War Forts, 1952-54; "Fort Ward Museum & Historic Site." A 1990 pamphlet issued by the City of Alexandria; "Fort Ward Museum & Historic Site," An undated pamphlet issued by the City of Alexandria; "Alexandria to Rebuild Civil War Fort Ward,"

The Washington Post, September 1, 1960; John Neary, "Beareded Bus Dweller Probes Fort's Ruins," *The Evening Star*, June 36, 1961; Jerry Kline, "Alexandria Restores Old Civil War Fort," *The Evening Star*, Aug 5, 1962; Everard Munsey, "Capital's Citadel of 1861 Being Restored as Park," *The Washington Post*, July 15, 1961; Thomas Oliver, "Ft. Ward Emerges in Changed Role," *The Evening Star*, June 26, 1967; "Fort Ward, Unscathed by War. Hit by Drought," *The Evening Star*, September 3, 1962; "Alexandria to Rebuild Civil War Fort Ward," *The Washington Post*, September 1, 1960.

38 James I. Robertson, Jr., *Civil War Sites in Virginia: A Tour Guide*. (Charlottesville, VA: The University Press of Virginia, 1982), 44.

39 Charles T. Jacobs, *Civil War Guide to Montgomery County, Maryland*. Rockville, MD: The Montgomery County Historical Society and the Montgomery County Civil War Round Table, 1983, 12; "A Walking Tour of Fort C.F. Smith Park," Pamphlet for Arlington Park (Arlington, VA: Arlington, n.d.); "Marking the Forts, *The Evening Star*, *Sunday Magazine*, September 11, 1966.

40 U.S., Work Projects Administration, Federal Writer's Program, *Washington, D.C.: A Guide to the Nation'Capital, American Guide Series*, Randall Bond Truett, Editor, New Revised Edition (Original edition published by The George Washington University of Washington, D. C. In 1942) (New York: Hastings House Publishers, 1968 Washington, DC: The George Washington University, 1942).

41 Daughters of the American Revolution, District of Columbia, State Historic Committee, *Historical Directory of the District of Columbia* (Washington, DC: State Historic Committee, District of Columbia, Daughters of the American Revolution, 1922), 74.

42 Theodore Dodge Gatchel, *Rambling Through Washington: An Account of Old and New Landmarks in Our Capital City* (Washington, DC: The Washington Journal, 1932), 227-28.

43 Theodore Dodge Gatchel, *Rambling Through Washington: An Account of Old and New Landmarks in Our Capital City* (Washington, DC: The Washington Journal, 1932), 234.

44 *25 Hikes In and Near Washington* (Washington, DC: Capital Transit Company, 1930s?), 11.

45 Information found in local phone books and maps of the area (1997).

Bibliography

MANUSCRIPT MATERIALS

Archives of the District of Columbia

Records of the District of Columbia

Central Classified Files: Engineer Department, (ED) Engineer Department Case Files, 1897-1955
#155186
#23181
#248515

Freedman Project, University of Maryland

Copies of Documents Collected for the Editing Project

Library of Congress

Periodical Sections

LC Newspapers
The Washington (Evening) Star, 1865-67
The Washington Post, April 1-May 25, 1898

Manuscript Division

Olmsted Associates Records
Frederick Law Olmsted Papers

National Archives

Textual Records

Record Group 42, Records of the Office of Public Buildings and Grounds

Entry 109, Newspaper Clippings, 1926-27, Box 5

General Correspondence, 307, Public Grounds: Extension of Park System:
Civil War Forts Parkway

Record Group 46, Records of the United States Senate

56th Congress, Committee Papers, Committee on Military Affairs, Sen 56A-F21,
Box 97

58th Congress, Sen 58A-E1, Box 38

59th Cong, Sen 59A-E1, Box 45

59th Congress, Sen 59A-E1, Box 54

60th Congress, Sen 60A-E1, Box 36;

67th Congress, Papers Re: to specific Bills and Resolutions, S.1-50, Box 1—S. 4

69th Congress, E-1, Box 39

Record Group 66, Records of the Commission on Fine Arts

E-17, Project Files, 1910-52

Forts: Fort Dupont—Water Tower
Fort Lincoln Cemetery, Prince Georges County, MD
Fort Reno—Water tower
Fort Stanton—Water Tower
Fort Stevens

Record Group 77, Records of the Office of the Chief of Engineers

Entry 18, Letters Received, 1826-66.

Entry 29, N & S Indexes to Series 30

Entry 30, Letters Sent, 1866-70

Entry 31, Name & Subject Index to Series 33

Entry 32, Register of Letters Received, 1866-67

Entry 33, Letters Received, 1866-67

Entry 34, Name & Subject Index to Series 36

Entry 36, Letters Received ("A" File), November 1867-November 1870

Entry 36, Letters Received, ("A" File), !867-70

Entry 40, Letters Sent Regarding Claims, 1866-70

Entry 45, Letters Received Regarding Claims, 1865-70.

Entry 99, Name and Subject Index to Series 103

Entry 102, Record Cards for General Correspondence, 1894-1923

Entry 103, General Correspondence, 1894-1923

Entry 127, Engineer Orders and Circulars, Orders, Issuances, 1811-1868

Entry 171, Land Papers, 1794-1916.

Entry 282, Registers of Claims Considered By the Chief of Engineers and the Chief of Topographical Bureau, 1860-94.

Entry 291, DeGrange Index, 1789-1889

Entry 572, Defenses of Washington, 1861-66, Correspondence Relating to Timber Claims, Statements of Timber Cut, Inspection Reports, and Requests for Compensation, 1862-65

Entry 574, Defenses of Washington, 1861-66, Land Releases, 1865.

Record Group 79, Records of the National Park Service

Entry 21, Annual & Quarterly Reports, 1913-42, NCR

Entry 21, Annual & Quarterly Reports, 1913-42, NCR, nothing

Entry 44, Records Concerning WPA Projects, 1935-43

E-119, Register of Battleground National Cemetery, (PI 166)

E121, Clippings, 1934-37

Records of the Branch of Recreation, Land Protection, and State Cooperation, Narrative Reports Concerning ECW (CCC) Projects in NPS Areas, 1933-35, District of Columbia

Record Group 92, Records of the Office of the Quartermaster General

Entry 225, Special Files, 1794-1926, Consolidated Correspondence File, 1794-1890

Entry 843, Claims and Related Papers for Damage to Property by Troops in the Service of the United States, 1861-65

Entry 1054, Miscellaneous Records Relating to Reservations and to Buildings, 1819-65

Claims files by Register Letter or Number and claims number

Record Group 94, Records of the Adjutant Generals Office, 1780s to 1917

Entry 12, Letters Received, 1805-89

Entry 25, Correspondence File, 1890-1917

Entry 26, Record Cards, 1890-1917

Entry 44, Orders and Circulars, 1797-1910

Entry 61, Returns of Departments, 1818-1916

Entry 226, Special File, 1790-1946

Entry 287, Miscellaneous File, 1800s-1917

Entry 289, General Information Index, 1794-1918

Entry 464, Reservation File, 1800s to 1916

Entry 465, Outline Index of Military Forts and Stations

Entry 501, Record and Pension Office, Document File, 1889-1904

National Archives Microfilm Pub., M617, Post Returns

Record Group 105, Records of the Bureau of Refugees, Freedmen, and Abandoned Lands

Entry 456, District of Columbia, Letters Received

Record Group 233, Records of the United States House of Representatives

67th Congress, Papers Accompanying Specific Bills and Resolutions, committee on district of Columbia, HR67A-D5, Box 99—H.R. 8792

Papers Accompanying Specific Bills and Resolutions, HR70A-D20, Box 375—H.R. 10556,

71st Congress, Papers Accompanying Specific Bills and Resolutions, Committee on Military Affairs, HR 1A-D20, Box 354—H.R. 11489

Record Group 328, Records of the National Capital Planning Commission

General Records, Parks & Recreation, Planning Files, 1924-67,

535, Parks & Recreation, Battery Kemble Park

535, Parks and Reservations, Fort Dupont Park

535, Parks and Reservations, Fort Foote

535, Parks and Reservations, Fort Totten Park

535, Parks and Reservations, Fort Totten Park—Incinerator No. 4

543-36, Civil War Forts, Preservation of

545-100, Fort Drive, Committee on

545-100, Fort Drive, Fort Drive #1

545-100, Fort Drive, Fort Drive #2

RG351, Record of the Government of the District of Columbia Land Records

Entry 51, General Files, 1924-68, 7-092, Box 329

Record Group 393, Records of United State Army Continental Commands, 1821-1920

>Preliminary Inventory 172, Part 1

>Department and Defenses of Washington and 22nd Army Corps, 1862-69,

>>Entry E-5375, Letters Sent, July 1864-March 1869,

>>Entry 5376, Letters Sent, Supplemental, 1866-69

>>Entry 5381, Registers of Letters Received, September 1862-March 1869

>>Entry 5382, Letters Received, September 1862-March 1869

>>Entry 5383, Letters Received (Unentered), 1863-67

>>Entry 5385, General Orders (Printed), Sept. 1862-Dec. 1867

>>Entry 5386, General Orders and Circulars, 1867-69

>>Entry 5395, Station Book of Troops, 1866-68

>>Entry 5408, Register of Information Furnished Relating to Claims, 1866-69

>>Entry 5423, Inventory and Inspection Reports, 1865-1868

>>Entry 5421, Letters Sent, 1865-69

>>Entry 5422, Endorsements Sent, 1865-69

>>Entry 5458, Register of Letters Received by the Chief Quartermaster, 1864-67

Preliminary Inventory 172, Part 1

>Defenses of Washington, August 1865-April 1866

>>Entry 695, Letters Sent, August 1865-April 1866

>>Entry 696, Endorsements, August 1865-April 1866

>>Entry 698, Special Orders and General Orders, August 1865-April 1866

>>Entry 699, Orders Received, August 1865-April 1866

>>Entry 701, Letters Sent and Circulars Issued by the Assistant Inspector General, August 1865-April 1866

>>Entry 702, Register of Inventory and Inspection Reports Forwarded and Returned, January 1865-April 1866

Cartographic and Architectural Archives—Maps, Drawings and Aerials

>RG-23   C&GS Topo Mapping of DC—index

RG-66   Special List, 1. District of Columbia

Metropolitan Area
> Fort Drive Parkway 26 items
> Fort Dupont 1
> Fort Reno 2
> Fort Stanton 1

> 5. Historic Maps of the District of Columbia, Maryland, and Virginia # 29, 30, 31

RG 77   Plan of Ft. Worth (1888), Drawer 170, Sheet 173 2

RG 79   National Capital Parks, Engineering Branch

> Fort DeRussy 55-92
> Battleground Cemetery 103-1 to
> Fort Drive Project - 100-1, 100.8-1
> Fort Stanton - 00.1-1
> Fort Stevens - 100.2-1
> Fort Bayard - 100.3-1
> Fort Carroll - 100.5-1
> Fort Baker - 100.4-1
> Battery Meade - 100.3-3
> Fort Reno - 100.6-1
> Fort Totten - 100.7-1

After 1984, Park Code - Fort Circle Parks, 832

NCP Numbered Drawings

> Fort Drive 100.2 - 100-52 (100-51, 100-50, 100-52),

> Fort Stanton 1-2, 1-3, 1-4, 1-8, 1-13, 1-15, 1-33

> Ft. Stevens 100.2-1, 2-2, 2-7, 2-9a, 2-10, 2-11 (100.2-1)

RG-328

NPC "Old Files"

> 1.9-203 - Aerial view of Washington and Virginia, photo, no date
> 37.3-18 - Anacostia River, US Engineer Reservation, 1932

NPC "New Files"

> 1927 Aerial Photos of DC

National Park Service, National Capital Region Office, Ohio Drive

Ed Fitzgerald to Rock Comstock, September 24, 1973, CRBIB Material, Fort Circle Parks, in Stephen Potters Office, National Park Service, National Capital Parks

Notebooks

Various Maps

National Register Collections, National Park Service, North Capital and H Streets, N.W.

Civil War Defenses of Washington National Register Nominations and miscellaneous similar type nominations

Rock Creek Park, National Park Service

Historical Files

U.S. Army Corps of Engineers, St. Louis District

"A" Site Fort Reno, Washington, D.C., Project Number-CO3DCO48401, March 1997, o   4.1.1

General Site History

U.S .Army Military History Institute, Carlisle Barracks, PA

Manuscript Section

Papers of Men who garrisoned forts in Washington, D.C.

Army War Student Papers relating to the Defenses of Washington, D.C.

NEWSPAPER ARTICLES

Arlington County, VA, Main Library

Newspaper Articles File

Martin Luther King Library

Newspaper Articles File

Virginiana Room, Fairfax Regional Library, Fairfax County, Virginia

Newspaper Articles File

Washington Historical Society

Newspaper Articles File

PUBLICATIONS AND OTHER STUDIES

Abbot, Henry L. A Biographical Memoir of John Gross Barnard." *Professional Memoirs, Corps of Engineers, United States Army and Engineer Department at Large*, 5, January-February 1913, 83-90.

Abbot, Henry Larcom. *Siege Artillery in the Campaigns Against Richmond, with Notes on the Fifteen-Inch Gun, Corps of Engineers Professional Paper No. 14.* Washington, DC: The Government Printing Office, 1867.

Adams, F. Colburn. *Siege of Washington, D. C. Written Expressly for Little People.* New York: Dick & Fitzgerald, Publishers, 1867.

The Advance upon Washington in July, 1864." *Southern Magazine*, 8, June 1871, 750-63.

Aide-Memoire to the Military Sciences. Framed from Contributions of Officers of the Different Services, and Edited by A Committee of the Corps of Royal Engineers in Dublin, 1845-1846. Three Volumes. London: John Weale, 1846-52.

Aide-Memoire to the Military Sciences. Framed from Contributions of the Different Services, and Edited by A Committee of the corps of Royal Engineers, 1847-1849. Volume II. Second Edition. London: John Weale, 1853.

Albro, Walt. The Forgotten Battle for the Capital (July 1864)." *Civil War Times Illustrated*, 32, January/February 1993, 40-43, 56-61.

Alexander, Edward Porter. "The Battle of Bull Run." *Scribner's Magazine*, 41, January 1907, 80-94.

Alexandria, VA—Jones Point on the Potomac." In Daughters of the American Revolution, District of Columbia, State Historic Committee. *Historical Directory of the District of Columbia.* Washington, DC: State Historic Committee, District of Columbia, Daughters of the American Revolution, 1922, 78.

"Alexandria to Rebuild Civil War Fort Ward." *The Washington Post*, Sept 1, 1960.

Allen, Herbert F. L. Allen. "Washington Is Defenseless." *The Evening Star*, Nov 18, 1934.

Ambrose, Stephen E. "Dennis Hart Mahan--A Profile." *Civil War Times Illustrated*, 2, November 1963, 30-35.

Ambrose, William S. *An Interpretive Earthworks Preservation Guide For Petersburg National Battlefield.* A Special Project submitted at Clemson University in partial fulfillment of the requirements for the degree of Master of Recreation and Park Administration, Department of Recreation and Park Administration. Prepared for U.S. Department of the Interior, National Park Service, Petersburg National Battlefield at Petersburg, Virginia. March 1976.

American Battle Monuments: A Guide to Military Cemeteries and Monuments Maintained by the American Battle Monuments Commission. Edited by Elizabeth Nishiura. Detroit, MI: Omnigraphics, Inc., 1989.

Ames, Mary Clemmer. *Ten Years In Washington: Life and Scenes in the National Capital, As A Woman Sees Them.* Hartford, CT: A.D. Worthington & Co., 1873.

"Area Forts: The Ramparts Once Watched." *The Washington Post,* June 25, 1967.

Armstrong, Cynthia Grant. "Fort Ward." *Northern Virginia Heritage,* 1, October 1979, 7-8, 20.

The Army and Navy Journal, Volumes 1-3.

"Army Road and Bridge Builders." In John D. Billings. *Hardtack and Coffee or The Unwritten Story of Army Life.* Boston: G.M. Smith and Co., 1887, 377-93.

Aubin, Henry. "District's Old Forts: Squirrels Man Ivied Ramparts." *The Washington Post,* Monday, December 28, 1970.

Babits, Lawrence E. "A Confederate Earthwork's Internal Structure." *Military Collector & Historian,* 41, Winter 1989, 194-98.

Barber, James G. *Alexandria in the Civil War.* Lynchburg, VA: H.E. Howard, Inc., 1988.

Barnard, John Gross. *The C.S.A. and the Battle of Bull Run.* New York: D. Van Nostrand, 1862.

Barnard, John Gross. *A Report on the Defenses of Washington, to the Chief of Engineers, U. S. Army, Corps of Engineers, Corps of Engineers Professional Paper No. 20.* Washington, DC: The Government Printing Office, 1871.

Barnard, John G., "The Use of Iron in Fortifications," *United States Service Magazine,* 1, (January 1, 1864, 25-31.

Barnard, John Gross and William F. Barry. *Report of the Engineer and Artillery Operations of the Army of the Potomac from Its Organization to the Close of the Peninsular Campaign.* New York: D. Van Nostrand, 1863..

Barthelmes, Wes. In Battery Kemble Park: Citizen Groups Hit Fort Drive Project." *The Washington Post,* April 27, 1955.

Battle, Stafford Levon. "In Defense of A Nation's Capital." *Washington Living*, May 1984, 50-53.

"Battle Fields, &c." In C.H. Ingram and John P. Church. *What You Most Want To Know. A Complete Guide and Directory, Prepared for the Members of the Grand Army of the Republic and Their Friends, Visiting the Washington National Encampment.* Washington, DC: John C. Parker, 1892, 16-18.

Battles and Leaders of the Civil War . . . Edited by Robert U. Johnson and Clarence C. Buell. 4 Volumes. New York: The Century Company, 1887-88.

Beach, William H. *The First New York (Lincoln) Cavalry from April 19, 1861 to July 7, 1865.* New York: The Lincoln Cavalry Association, 1902.

"Beauty Duty Sought for 16 Old Forts.." *The Washington Post*, May 7, 1965.

Bell, J. Franklin. "City Engineering in Washington." *The Military Engineer*, 19, September-October 1927, 359-63.

Benedict, Grenville. *Army Life in Virginia: Letters from the Twelfth Vermont Regiment and Personal Experience of Volunteer Service in the War of the Union, 1862-63.* Burlington, VT: Free Press Association, 1895.
Besson, F.S. "The Street System of a Modern City." *The Military Engineer*, 15, March- April 1923, 1-5-11.

Billings, Elden E. "Military Activities in Washington in 1861." *Records of the Columbia Historical Society of Washington, D.C.,*, 1960-1962, 131-33.

Bissell, Lewis. *The Civil War Letters of Lewis Bissell: A Curriculum.* Edited by Mark Olcott and David Lear. Washington, DC: The Field School Educational Foundation Press, 1981.

Blanding, Stephen F. *In the Defenses of Washington or Sunshine in A Soldier's Life.* Providence, RI: E.L. Freeman, 1889.

Bowen, John. *Battlefields of the Civil War: A State-by-State Guide.* London: Chartwell Books, Inc., 1986.

Brackenbury, Charles B. *Field Works, Their Technical Construction and Tactical Application.* London: Kegan Paul, Trench & Co., 1888.

Bradwell, I.G. "On to Washington." *Confederate Veteran*, 36, March 1928, 95-96.

Brager, Bruce L. "Fort Stevens--Lincoln Under Fire." *Northern Virginian*, 12, July-August 1982, 22-24.

Brewer, James H. *The Confederate Negro: Virginia's Craftsman and Military Laborers, 1861-1865.* Durham, NC: Duke University Press, 1969.

Brewer, Roy C. "Fort Scott—Past, Present, and Future." *The Arlington Historical Magazine*, 3, October 1965, 40-47.

Brialmont, Alexis Henri. *Hasty Entrenchments.* Translated by Charles A. Empson. London: Henry S. King & Co., 1872.

Brice, Martin. *Forts and Fortresses: From the Hillforts of Prehistory to Modern Times—the Definitive Visual Account of the Science of Fortification.* New York: Facts On File, Inc., 1990.

"Brightwood School Site Shift Planned." *The Washington Post*, September 16, 1949.

Brooks, Noah. *Mr. Lincoln's Washington: The Civil War Dispatches of Noah Brooks.* Edited by P.J. Staudenraus. New York: Thomas Yoseloff, Publisher, 1967.

Brooks, Noah. *Washington, D. C. in Lincoln's Time.* Edited with a new commentary by Herbert Mitgang. Chicago, IL: Quadrangle Books, 1971.

Brown, Carey H. "The Scope and Importance of City Planning." *The Military Engineer*, 20, September-October 1928, 413-15.

Brown, Glen. *Papers Relating to the Improvement of Washington City.* Washington, D.C.: The Government Printing Office, 1901.

Brown, J. Willard. *The Signal Corps USA in the War of the Rebellion.* Published by the U.S. Veterans Signal corps Association. Reprint. New York: New York Times, Co., 1974.

Brown, Leonard E. *Forts DeRussy, Stevens, and Totten; General Background.* Washington, DC: Division of History, Office of Archeology and Historic Preservation, National Park Service, 1968.

Brown, Leonard E. *National Capital Parks: Fort Stanton, Fort Foote, Battery Ricketts.* Washington, DC: Office of History and Historic Architecture, Eastern Service Center, National Park Service, 1970.

Browning, Robert S., III. *"Two if by Sea: The Development of American Coastal Defense Policy.* Westport, CT: Greenwood Press, 1983.

Bryan, Wilhelmus Bogart. Compiler. *Bibliography of the District of Columbia being A List of Books, Maps, and Newspapers, including Articles in Magazines and Other Publications to 1898.* Washington, GPO, 1900.

Bryan, Wilhelmus Bogart. *A History of the National Capital from its foundation through the Period of the Adoption of the Organic Act.* Volume II. *1815-1878.* New York: The Macmillan Company, 1916, 539-40.

Buchanan, James. *The Works of James Buchanan.* Edited by John Bassett Moore. Reprint. New York: , 1960.

Buckholtz, Louis von. *On Infantry, Camp Duty, Field Fortification, and Coast Defence.* Washington, DC: Selmar Siebert, 1860.

"Bunker Mentality," *City Paper,* January 13-19, 1995.

Bushong, William. *Historic Resource Study: Rock Creek Park - District of Columbia.* Washington, DC: The Government Printing Office, 1990.

Butler, Benjamin F. *Private and Official Correspondence of General Benjamin F. Butler during the Period of the Civil War . . .* 5 Volumes. Norwood, MA: Plimpton Press, 1917.

Calvin, Rita A. Compiler. *Selected Theses and Dissertations on the Washington, D.C. Region.* Washington, DC: Center for Washington, DC: Center for Washington Area Studies, George Washington University, 1982.

Caemmerer, H.Paul. "The Corps of Engineers and the Capital City." *The Military Engineer,* 45, May-June 1953, 206-10.

Caemmerer, H.Paul. *A Manual on the Origin and Development of Washington; Senate Document No. 178,* 75th Congress, 3rd Session. Washington, DC: GPO, 1939.

Caemmerer, H.Paul. "Topographic Features Relating to the Plan of Washington, D.C." *The Military Engineer,* 45, January-February 1952, 15-19.

Caemmerer, H.Paul. *Washington the National Capital, Senate Report No. 332,* 71st Congress, 3rd Session. Washington, DC: GPO, 1932.

"Calendar No. 1101," *Senate Report No. 1036,* 68th Congress, 2nd Session, February 3, 1925.

Carper, Robert L. *Historic Structure Report, Administrative and Architectural Data Sections, Fort Washington Main Fort/Ravelin.* Denver, CO: Denver Service Center, The National Park Service, 1982.

Cartwright, William H., Jr. with Louise E. Goeden. Abridged by William M. Offutt. *The Military District of Washington 1942-1945.* Bethesda, MD: Published by the Author, Printed by Brother's Printing, 1995.

Chandler, David G. "Haunted Acres: Visiting Battlefields." *History Today*, 26, November 1976, 743-48.

Chesney, Charles C. *On the Value of Fortresses and Fortified Positions in Defensive Operations.* Second Edition, Revised. London: Byfield, Stanford & Co., 1868.

Churchman, Deborah. "Searching for the Civil War (Report from the Forts)." *The Washington Post*, Weekend, October 23, 1981.

"Civil War Forts." In *Historic Northern Virginia Buildings and Places.* Published by the Northern Virginia Regional Planning and Economic Development Commission. n.d.

Civil War Round Table of the District of Columbia, "Washington Needs The Fort Memorial Freeway," Pamphlet, (1953?).

"Civil War's Fort Marcy Slated to Become Park," *The Washington Post and Times Herald*, Thursday, March 13, 1958.

Clinton, Amy Cheney. "Historic Fort Washington." *Maryland Historical Magazine*, 32, September 1937, 228-47.

Clopton, Willard. "Park Service Weighs Future of Fort Drive," *The Washington Post*, Monday, April 30, 1962;

Coggins, Jack. "The Engineers Played a Key Role in Both Armies." *Civil War Times Illustrated*, 3, January 1965, 40-47.

Colbert, Leo Otis. "Earliest Maps of Washington, D.C." *The Military Engineer*, 61, July-August 1949, 247-50.

Colket, Meredith B. "The Public Records of the District of Columbia." *Records of the Columbia Historical Society of Washington, D.C.*, Vols. 48-49, 1949, 281-99.

Commemoration Ceremony on The One Hundreth Anniversary of the Battle of Fort Stevens at Fort Stevens Pamphlet. Washington, D.C. , July 11, 1964.

"Commemoration of Certain Military Historic Events, and for Other Purposes." *House Report No. 1525*, 71st Congress, 2nd Session, May 19, 1930, 24.

Cooling, Benjamin Franklin, III. "Civil War Deterrent: Defenses of Washington." *Military Affairs* (hereafter referred to as *MA*), 29, Winter 1965-66, 164-78.

Cooling, Benjamin Franklin, III. "Defending Washington During the Civil War." *Records of the Columbia Historical Society of Washington, D.C.*, Vol. 71-72, 1971-72, 314-37.

Cooling, Benjamin Franklin. *Jubal Early's Raid On Washington 1864*. Baltimore, MD: The Nautical and Aviation Publishing Company of America, 1989.

Cooling, Benjamin Franklin, III. *Symbol, Sword, and Shield: Defending Washington During the Civil War*. Second Edition. Shippensburg, PA: White Mane Publishing Company, Inc., 1991.

Cooling, Benjamin Franklin, III and Walton H. Owen, II. *Mr. Lincoln's Forts: A Guide to the Civil War Defenses of Washington*. Shippensburg, PA: White Mane Publishing Company, 1988.

"County Seeks to Preserve Ft. Reynolds," *Washington Post*, Sept 9, 1954.

Cowdrey, Albert E. *A City for the Nation: The Army Engineers and the Building of Washington, D.C., 1798-1967*. Washington, DC: The Government Printing Office, 1979.

Cox, James A. "Fort Delaware on the Water." *Civil War Times Illustrated*, 32, July-August 1993, 20-24, 26, 54.

Cox, William Van Zandt. "The Defenses of Washington—General Early's Advance on the Capital and the Battle of Fort Stevens, July 11 and 12, 1864." *Records of the Columbia Historical Society, Washington*, 1901, Vol. IV, 135-65.

Cox, William Van Zandt. *The Defenses of Washington—General Early's Advance on the Capital and the Battle of Fort Stevens, July 11 and 12, 1864* 1-31. Pamphlet.

Craighill, William P. *The Army Officer's Pocket Companion*. New York: D. Van Nostrand, 1863.

Cramer, John Henry. *Lincoln Under Enemy Fire: The Complete Account of His Experiences During Early's Attack on Washington*. Baton Rouge, LA: Louisiana State University Press, 1948.

Cromie, Alice. *A Tour Guide to the Civil War*. Third Edition, Revised and Updated. Nashville, TN: Rutledge Hill Press, 1990.

Cronin, Gerald E. "The Attacks on Our National Capital." *Infantry Journal*, 11, September/October 1914, 214-20.
Crouch, Howard R. *Relic Hunter: The Field Account of Civil War Sites, Artifacts, and Hunting*. Fairfax, VA: SCS Publications, 1978.

Crowell, Elizabeth A., Dennis Knepper and Marcia Miller. *Archaeological Investigations of Fort C.F. Smith*. July 1987. Engineering-Science, Inc., Washington, DC., 1987.

Cullum, George W. *Systems of Military Bridges in Use by the United States Army . . .* New York: D. Van Nostrand, 1863.

Cummings, Maizie Jean. ˙ *Battleground National Cemetery; An Example of A Victorian Mourning Area*. George Washington University, August 24, 1990.

Curry, W.W. "To the Potomac." Edited by Paula Mitchell Marks.   *Civil War Times Illustrated*, 28, September/October 1989, 24-25, 59-65.

Curtis, William T.S. "Cabin John Bridge." *Records of the Columbia Historical Society of Washington, D. C.*, 2, 1899, 293-307.

Cutts, James Madison. *Gun and Mortar Batteries, 1897 to 1905, Fort Washington, Maryland: Structural Condition Survey* . 2 Volumes. Washington, DC: Raymond, Parish, Pine and Plavnick, Planning and Community Development Consultants, 1975?.

"D.C.'s Dwindling Tax Sources." *The Washington News*, January 24, 1947.

Dana, Charles A. "Early's Raid on Washington." In Charles A. Dana. "Reminiscences of Men and Events of the Civil War." Part VII. *McClure's Magazine*, 11, May 1898, 38-40.

Daughters of the American Revolution, District of Columbia, State Historic Committee, *Historical Directory of the District of Columbia*. Washington, DC: State Historic Committee, District of Columbia, Daughters of the American Revolution, 1922.

David, Elizabeth S. "Fort Willard and the Defenses of Washington." *Fairfax Chronicles*, 10, November 1986-January 1987, 1, 4-5.

Davis, David G. "Fort Ward, Defending Washington." *Castle* (Ft. Belvoir, VA), 52, February 27, 1987, 7.

Davis, Henry E. "Ninth and F Streets and Thereabout." *Records of the Columbia Historical Society of Washington, D.C.*, Vol. 5, 1902.

Davis, William C. *The Battle at Bull Run: A History of the First Major Campaign of the Civil War*. Garden City, NY: Doubleday, 1977.

Day, Gene Hart. "Washington's Scenic Masterpiece—A Highway of Forts." *American Motorist*, February 1933, 16-17, 32-33.

de Trobriand, Comte Regis. *The Life and Memoirs of Comte Regis de Trobriand Major-General in the Army of the United States by His Daughter Marie Caroline Post.* New York: E.P. Dutton & Company, 1910.

de Trobriand, Comte Regis. *Our Noble Blood: The Civil War Letters of Major-General Regis de Trobriand.* Translated by Nathalie Chartrain. Edited by William B. Styple. Kearny, NJ: Belle Grove Publishing Co., 1997.

"Defense of Washington." Chapter Three in U.S., Engineer School. *Engineer Operations in Past Wars.* 2 Parts. Fort Humphreys, VA: Engineer School, 1926, Part I, pages 23-35.

"Defenses of Washington." In DeB. Randolph Keim. *Keim's Illustrated Hand-Book. Washington and Its Environs: A Descriptive and Historical Hand-Book to the Capital of the United States of America.* Fourth Edition—Corrected to July, 1874. Washington, DC: For the Compiler, 1874, 232-33.

"The Defenses of Washington." In Noah Brooks. *Mr. Lincoln's Washington: Selections from the Writings of Noah Brooks Civil War Correspondent.* Edited by P.J. Staudenraus. New York: Thomas Yoseloff, 1967, 197-99.

"The Defenses of Washington During the War." *The Evening Star,* October 9, 1902.

Development of the United States Capital: Address Delivered in the Auditorium of the United States Chamber of Commerce Building, Washington, D.C., at Meetings Held to discuss the Development of The National Capital April 25-26, 1929; House Document No. 35, 71st Congress, 1st Session. Washington, DC: GPO, 1930.

Devlin, Raymond A. "Report of Civilian Conservation Corps Operations in the National Capital Parks, October 15, 1933-June 30, 1942." Washington, D.C. National Capital Parks, 1950.

Dey, Richard A., Jr. "The Defenses of Washington, D.C., United States of America: Yesterday and Today." *Army Digest,* 24, August 1969, 18-21.

Dickman, William J. *Battery Rodgers at Alexandria, Virginia.* Manhattan, KS: MA/AH Publishing, 1980.

"The Dismantled Forts," *The Evening Star,* Thursday, Sept. 28, 1865.

District of Columbia. CW Centennial Comm. *Study in Patriotism, 1861-1865.* Washington, D.C.: n.p., 1965?

"District, Park Service Clash Over Highway vs. Parkway." *The Washington Post,* April 2, 1961.

"District's Old Forts," *Washington Post*, Dec. 10, 1970.

Dodge, Grenville Mellon. "Use of Blockhouses During the Civil War." *Annals of Iowa*, 6, January 1904, 297-301.

Donn, John W. "With the Army of the Potomac From the Defences of Washington to Harrison's Landing." In District of Columbia Commander, The Military Order of the Loyal Legion of the United States. *War Papers*, Paper 22.

Donnelly, Ralph W. "Fort Branch on the Roanoke." *Periodical: The Journal of the Council on America's Military Past* (formerly Council on Abandoned Military Posts), 9, Fall 1977, 30-38.

Douglass, Frederick. *The Frederick Douglass Papers*. Series One. Speeches, Debates and Interviews, 1847-95. 5 Volumes. New Haven, CT: Yale University Press, 1979-92.

Douglas, Howard. *Observations on Modern Systems of Fortification, Including that proposed by M. Carnot, and a Comparison of the Polygonal with the Bastion System; To which is Added, Some Reflections on Entrenched Positions, and a Tract on the Naval, Littoral, and Internal Defence of England*. London: J. Murray, 1859.

Downs, Terrance. "Sunset on the Palisade." *Potomac: T.W.P. Magazine*, February 5, 1978.

Doyle John T. "Fort Lincoln : history and construction." November 13, 1933. This paper was prepared as part of Doyle's initiation into Phi Mu an engineering honor society. Records of Phi Mu University of Maryland at College Park Libraries.

Duane, James C. "History of the Bridge Equipage in the United States Army." In Printed Papers of the Essay on Club of the Corps of Engineers. Willet's Point, New York: Battalion Press, 1872, I, No. 1.

Duane, James C. *Manual for Engineer Troops*. New York: D. Van Nostrand, 1862.

Duffy, Christopher. *Fire and Stone: The Science of Fortress Warfare 1660-1860*. London: David and Charles, 1975.

Duffy, Christopher. "Touring a Fortress," *Fire and Stone: The Science of Fortress Warfare 1660-1860*. London: David and Charles, 1975, 198-200.

Duryee Sacket L. *A Historical Summary of the Work of the Corps of Engineers in Washington, D. C. and Vicinity, 1852-1952*. Washington, DC: Washington Engineer District, 1952.

Dwight, Henry O. "In the Trenches: Each Man His Own Engineer." *Civil War Times Illustrated*, 4, October 1965, 4-7, 30-31.

Early, Jubal A. "The Advance on Washington in 1864." *Southern Historical Society Papers*, 9, 1881, 297-312.

Early, Jubal A. "General Barnard's Report on the Defences of Washington, in July 1864." *Southern Magazine* (Baltimore), 10, June 1872, 716-24.

"Early's Raid on Washington." *The Republic*, Vol., VIII, No. 3, March 1877.

Edelin, William B. "The District of Columbia in the Civil War." M.A. thesis, Howard University, 1925.

Edgerton, Joseph S. "Capital's War Defense Revealed in Winter." *The Washington Star*, Feb 27, 1938.

Edmonds, James E. "The Engineers in Grant's Campaigns of 1864-5." *Royal Engineer's Journal*, 52, September 1938, 452-54.

Eisen, Jack. "Unreconstructed Rebels Will Not Buy Civil War Fort Marcy for Parkway," *The Washington Post*, April 3, 1958.;

Eisen, Jack. "Viewing Washington's Forts." *The Washington Post*, April 3, 1984.

Eisterhold, John A. "Fort Heiman: Forgotten Fortress." *The West Tennessee Historical Society Papers*, 28, 1974, 43-54.

Ellis, John B., *Sights and Secrets of the National Capital; A Work Descriptive of Washington and All Its Phases*. New York: United States Publishing Company, 1869.

Eliot, Charles W., II. "Planning Washington and Its Environs." *City Planning*, 3, July 1927, 3-19.

Eliot, Regina D. "The Fort Drive." *The Washingtonian*, November 1930, 18-19.

"Engineer Equipment." In Francis A. Lord. *Civil War Collector's Encyclopedia*. Harrisburg, PA: Stackpole Books, 1963, 91-99.

"Engineer Equipment." In Francis A. Lord. *Civil War Collector's Encyclopedia*. Volume 2. W. Columbia, SC: Lord Americana & Research, Inc., 1975, 46-49.

"The Engineers." In Jack Coggins. *Arms and Equipment of the Civil War*. Garden City, NY: Doubleday, 1962, 99-105.

Epling, Jimmie. "Pioneer Tools." *Camp Chase Gazette*, 15, October 1987, 18-19; November-December 1987, 22-23.

Evans, Thomas J. and James M. Moyer. *Mosby's Confederacy: A Guide to the Roads and Sites of John Singleton Mosby*. Shippensburg, PA: White Mane Publishing Company, Inc., 1991.

Everhart, William C. *Vicksburg National Military Park, Mississippi*. Washington, DC: The Government Printing Office, 1954.

Everly, Elaine Cutler. "The Freedmen's Bureau in the National Capital." Ph.D. dissertation, George Washington University, 1972.

Fairfax County and the War Between the States. Official Publication of the Fairfax County Civil War Centennial Commission. Fairfax County, VA: Office of Comprehensive Planning, Fairfax County, 1987. "Fairfax Official Recalls how >Sit-In' Saved Historic Fort From Bulldozers, *The Washington Post*, July 30, 1963.

Farwell, Byron. *Ball's Bluff: A Small Battle and Its Long Shadow*. McLean, VA: EPM Publications, Inc., 1990.

Faust, Patricia L. "Freedmen's Bureau," in *Historical Times Illustrated Encyclopedia of the Civil War*. New York: Harper & Row, Publishers, 1986,. 290

Fawcett, Waldon. "The Longest Concrete Bridge in the World (Taft Bridge Over Rock Creek Park)." *American Exporter*, 62, December 1908, 87-89.

Featherstonhaugh, A. "Notes on the Defences of Petersburg." In *Great Britain, Army, Corps of Royal Engineers. Papers on Subjects Connected with the Duties of the Royal Engineers . . .* Woolwich, England: W.P. Jackson, 1839-76, New Series, 14, 1865, 190-94.

Fernald, Granville. Compiler. *The Story of the First Defenders, District of Columbia, Pennsylvania, Massachusetts Wash, DC*. Washington, D.C.: Clarence E. Davis, 1892.

Fiebeger, Gustav J. *A Textbook on Field Fortification*. Third Edition. New York: John Wiley & Sons, 1913.

"Field Fortifications." In Egbert L. Viele. *Hand-book for Active Service; Containing Practical Instructions in Campaign Duties, for the Use of Volunteers*. New York: D. Van Nostrand, 1861, 92-148.

"Field Entrenchments." *Army and Navy Journal*, 6, November 7, 1868, 184-85.

Fine, Lenore and Jesse A. Remington. *The Corps of Engineers: Construction in the United States.* Washington, DC The Government Printing Office, 1972.

Fisher, Perry G. And Linda J. Lear. Compilers and Editors. *A Selected Bibliography for Washington Studies and Descriptions of Major Local Collections, George Washington University Studies Number Eight.* Washington, DC: George Washington University, May, 1981.

Floyd, Dale E. "Army Engineers in the Civil War." In *Military Engineering and Technology: Paper s Presented at the 1982 American Military Institute Annual Meeting, U. S. Army Engineer Center, Fort Belvoir, Virginia.* Manhattan, KS: MA/AH Publishing, 1984, 23-32.

Floyd, Dale E. "The Corps of Engineers' Role in Coast Defense." In Dale E. Floyd. *Defending America's Coasts, 1775-1950: A Bibliography.* Washington, DC: The Government Printing Office, 1997, xi-xxvi.

Floyd, Dale E. *Defending America's Coasts, 1775-1950: A Bibliography.* Washington, DC: The Government Printing Office, 1997.

Floyd, Dale E. *Military Fortifications: A Selective Bibliography; Bibliographies and Indexes in Military Studies, Number 4.* Westport, CT: Greenwood Publishing Group, Inc., 1992.

Floyd, Dale E. "The Place of Fortifications in the Civil War," *Midwest Region Battlefield Update* (National Park Service), 3, May 1994, 2-3.

Floyd, Dale E. "The Place of Fortifications in the Civil War with Emphasis on Kentucky," *Heritage Spirit* (Kentucky Heritage Council), 3, September-October 1994, 9-12.

Floyd, Dale E. "U.S. Army Officers in Europe, 1815-1861." In *Proceedings of the Citadel Conference on War and Diplomacy 1977.* Edited by David H. White and John W. Gordon. Charleston, SC: The Citadel, 1979, 26-30.

"For Military Park," *The Evening Star*, Thursday, December 20, 1906.

"For Park At Fort Stevens," *The Washington Post*, December 21, 1906.

Forman, Stephen M. "Driving Tour: Sites to See in Washington." *Blue & Gray Magazine*, 13, Spring 1996, 56-61.

Forman, Stephen M. "The General's Tout: A Glimpse of Wartime Washington." *Blue & Gray Magazine*, 13, Spring 1996, 8-18, 20, 22, 46-55.

Forman, Stephen M. *A Guide to Civil War Washington*. Washington, DC: Elliott & Clark Publishers, 1995.

"Fort Bayard Park Has Much History," *The Washington Post*, July 13, 1930.

Fort Circle Parks, Civil War Defenses of Washington, D.C. Brochure. Washington, D.C.: Parks and History Association in cooperation with the National Park Service, 1993.

"Fort Drive," *The Evening Star*, Saturday, November 16, 1940.

"Fort Drive." *The Washington Post*, January 29, 1947.

"The Fort Drive." *The Washington Star*, May 23, 1896.

"The Fort Drive, Major Powell's Proposed Circuit of the War Time Defenses, Historic Remains About This City, How Washington Was Defended During the Rebellion, Memories of the War: The Proposition of Engineer Commissioner Powell to establish a new drive-way through the suburbs of Washington to be called "Fort Drive," *The Evening Star*, May 23, 1896.

"Fort Drive Sought for Centennial." *The Washington Post*, March 1, 1958.

"Fort Drive Up for Study Today." *The Washington Post*, March 20, 1947.

"Fort Dupont Park Suits Under Way," The *Evening Star*, December 11, 1935;

"Fort Foote, "*The Evening Star*, June 1, 1926;

"Fort Foote Ordered Delayed," *The Evening Star*, June 12, 1926;

"Fort Foote Wanted in D. C. Park System," *Evening Star*, April 29, 1924

"Fort Marcey's Guns Protected Bridge Entering Georgetown Pike," *Fairfax Herald*, February 25, 1972, 7.

Fort Myer Post. *The History of Fort Myer, Virginia*. 100th Anniversary Issue, June 1863.

Fort Myer, VA, Administrative History and Records Listings Page; *A Narrative History of Fort Myer Virginia*. Falls Church, VA: Litho-Print Press, 1954?.

Fort Myer, Va., (originally Fort Whipple) Historical Sketch, 1934.

"Fort Sites Eyed for Future Use." *The Washington Post*, Friday, October 2, 1964.

Fine, Lenore
ington, DC T

ur s mg Pouts of Historic Interest,
Published by the Committee,

Fisher, Perry
Studies and L
Washington, 1

Floyd, Dale I
Presented at
Belvoir, Virgi

= Congress, 1st Session, June

Floyd, Dale E
Coasts, 1775-

200 538

Floyd, Dale E
ment Printing

en of Alexandria; "Fort Ward

Floyd, Dale E
Studies, Numl

er 3, 1962.

Floyd, Dale E.
Park Service),

ber 14, 1863, 182.

Remembers . .: The History,

Floyd, Dale E.
(Kentucky Her

m n Washington 1861-1862. Manassas,

Floyd, Dale E.
War and Diplo
1979, 26-30.

Sketch Book By Viator. New

"For Military P

at February 25, 1947.

"For Park At F

and Its Bearing on Tactics. Lon-

Forman, Steph
56-61.

Edited by Ira Berlin, Barbara
N The Blue & Gray Press,

Forman, Step
13, Spring 19

In John Clagett Proctor. Editor.
NDQ, 398-413

S. *Frobel of Wilton Hill in Virginia.* McLean, VA: EPM

ivil War in the Evolution of War." *Army Quarterly*, 26 July

ashington Herald, August 14, 1938.

Asked by D C " *The Washington Herald*, August 25, 1938.

Washington Post, August 6, 1987.

Washington Soldiers' Home & Colony, 1891-1971 : over f veterans Compiled by Muriel Furney for Washington bmatory Industries Printing Plant, 1974(?).

hen's Aid Societies in the District of Columbia, 1860-1870."

emy of the United States . . . Volunteers and Militia of the New York D Van Nostrand, 1859.

McLean, 13, February 1975, 8, 12-13.

Washington: An Accout of Old and New Landmarks in Our tJournal, 1932

)ring the American Civil War: A Vision for WWI Leaders." ncks, PA. April 1991.

man (Washington-Lee High School), 12 (3), Spring 1950,

*berations Against the Defense of Charleston Harbor in *Ind. the Demolition of Fort Sumter, the Reduction of Forts *Ordnance, Fortifications, etc., Corps of Engineer Profes-* rad. 1865.

*td States Engineer Department, of the Siege and Reduction *ad April, 1862. Corps of Engineers Paper on Practical* n, 1862.

"Fort Stevens," Editorial in *The Washington Star*, March 27, 1911.

"Fort Stevens at Brightwood." In Washington, D.C., Committee on Marking Points of Historic Interest, 1921. *Points of Historic Interest in the National Capital*. Washington, DC: Published by the Committee, 1921, 22.

"Fort Stevens Battle Marked by G.A.R. Unit." *The Washington Post*, July 11, 1938.

"Ft. Stevens Falls in Building Drive," *The Evening Star*, May 16, 1925;

"Fort Stevens-Lincoln National Military Park," *Senate Document No. 433*, 57th Congress, 1st Session, June 26, 1902. Washington, DC: The Government Printing Office, 1902.

"Fort Stevens, Near Washington City." *Confederate Veteran*, 8, December 1900, 538.

"Fort Ward Museum & Historic Site." A 1990 pamphlet issued by the City of Alexandria; "Fort Ward Museum & Historic Site," An undated pamphlet issued by the City of Alexandria;

"Fort Ward, Unscathed by War, Hit by Drought," *The Evening Star*, September 3, 1962;

"Fortification—Land Defences—Profiles." *Army & Navy Journal*, I, November 14, 1863, 182.

"The Fortifications of Washington." In Joseph Mills Hanson. *Bull Run Remembers . . .: The History, Traditions and Landmarks of the Manassas (Bull Run) Campaigns before Washington 1861-1862*. Manassas, VA: National Capitol Publishers, Inc., 1961, pages 29-30.

"The Forts." Chapter XXXV In Joseph Varnum, Joseph. *The Washington Sketch Book*. By Viator. New York: Mohun, Ebbs & Hough, 1864, 267-73

"Fowler to Stick To His Figures on Fort Drive Cost." *The Washington Post*, February 25, 1947.

Fraser, Thomas. *Field Entrenching: Its Application on the Battle-Field and Its Bearing on Tactics*. London: Mitchell, 1879.

Free at Last: A Documentary History of Slavery, Freedom and the Civil War. Edited by Ira Berlin, Barbara J. Fields, Steven F. Miller, Joseph P. Reidy, and Leslie S. Rowland. Edison, NJ: The Blue & Gray Press, 1997.

Fries, Amos A. "The District of Columbia in the World War." Chapter 38. In John Clagett Proctor. Editor. *Washington, Past and Present: A History*. 4 Volumes. New York: Lewis, 1930, 398-413.

Frobel, Anne S. *The Civil War Diary of Anne S. Frobel of Wilton Hill in Virginia.* McLean, VA: EPM Publications, Inc., 1992.

Fuller, John .F.C. "The Place of the American Civil War in the Evolution of War." *Army Quarterly*, 26 July 933, 316-25.

"Funds Asked to Construct Fort Drive." *The Washington Herald*, August 14, 1938.

"Funds for fort -to-Fort Drive And Health Unit Asked by D.C." *The Washington Herald*, August 25, 1938.

Furman, Lloyd. "1865 Beltway of Forts." *The Washington Post*, August 6, 1987.

Furney, Muriel. *A Comprehensive History of Washington Soldiers' Home & Colony, 1891-1971 : over eighty years of service to our State's disabled veterans.* Compiled by Muriel Furney for Washington Soldiers' Home & Colony. Monroe, WA: Reformatory Industries Printing Plant, 1974(?).

Fry, Gladys Marie. "The Activities of the Freedmen's Aid Societies in the District of Columbia, 1860-1870." M.A. thesis, Howard University, 1954.

Gardner, Charles K., *A Dictionary of . . . the Army of the United States . . . Volunteers and Militia of the States . . . and of the Navy and Marine Corps.* New York: D. Van Nostrand, 1859.

Gaskins, Ceres H. "Now and Then." *Sound of McLean*, 13, February 1975, 8, 12-13.

Gatchel, Theodore Dodge. *Rambling Through Washington: An Accout of Old and New Landmarks in Our Capital City.* Washington, DC: The Washington Journal, 1932.

Gates, John M. "Evolution of Entrenchments During the American Civil War: A Vision for WWI Leaders." Student paper, Army War College, Carlisle Barracks, PA, April 1991.

Gibson, Dave. "The Arlington Lines." *The Penman* (Washington-Lee High School), 12 (3), Spring 1950, 9-10, 48-51.

Gillmore, Quincy A. *Engineer and Artillery Operations Against the Defense of Charleston Harbor in 1863: Comprising the Descent Upon Morris Island, the Demolition of Fort Sumter, the Reduction of Forts Wagner and Gregg, with Observations on Heavy Ordnance, Fortifications, etc., Corps of Engineer Professional Paper No. 16.* New York: D. Van Nostrand, 1865.

Gillmore, Quincy A. *Official Report to the United States Engineer Department, of the Siege and Reduction of Fort Pulaski, Georgia, February, March, and April, 1862, Corps of Engineers Paper on Practical Engineering No. 8.* New York: D. Van Nostrand, 1862.

Gillmore, Quincy A. *Supplementary Report to Engineer and Artillery Operations Against the Defences of Charleston Harbor in 1863*. New York: D. Van Nostrand, 1868.

Gordon, Martin K. "The Black Militia in the District of Columbia, 1867-1898." *Records of the Columbia Historical Society of Washington, D.C.*, 1971-72, 411-20.

Gordon, Martin K. "The Origins of the Anacostia River Improvement Project: The Role of the Army Corps of Engineers." *Soundings: A Journal of Writings and Studies of the Potomac River Basin Consortium*, 4, Spring 1987, 10-18.

Grafton, Henry D. "Field Fortification." Chapter II in Henry D. Grafton. *A Treatise on the Camp and March with Which Is Connected the Construction of Field Works and Military Bridges. With an Appendix of Artillery Ranges, &c. for Use of Volunteers and Militia in the United States*. Boston: W.P. Fetridge and Co., 1854, 23-38.

Graham, Roy Eugene. "Federal Fort Architecture in Texas During the Nineteenth Century." *Southwestern Historical Quarterly*, 74, October 1970, 165-88.

Grant, Ulysses S. *The Papers of Ulysses S. Grant*. Edited by John Y. Simon. Multivolume. Carbondale, IL: Southern Illinois University Press, 1967-.

Grant, Ulysses S, III. "The L'Enfant Plan and Its Evolution." *Records of the Columbia Historical Society of Washington, D. C.*, 33, 1929, I-23.

Grant, Ulysses S, III. "The National Capital: Reminiscences of Sixty-Five Years." *Records of the Columbia Historical Society of Washington, D. C.*, 57-59, 1959, 1-15.

Grant, Ulysses S, III. "Planning the National Capital: Objectives and Problems of Attainment." *Transactions of the American Society of Civil Engineers*, 117, 1952, 119-30.

Grant, Ulysses S, III, et al. *The Development of the National Capital and Its Environs*. Washington, D.C.: National Conference of City Planning, 1928.

Green, Constance M. *The Secret City: A History of Race Relations in the Nation's Capital*. Princeton, NJ: Princeton University Press, 1967.

Green, Constance M. *Washington Village and Capital 1800-1878*. And *Washington Capital City 1879-1950*. Princeton, NJ: Princeton University Press, 1962 and 1963.

Grenville, John H. *A Study of Embrasures: Shapes and Methods of Construction 1820-65; Manuscript Report Number 369*. Ottawa, Canada: Parks Canada, 1980.

Griess, Thomas E. "Dennis Hart Mahan: West Point Professor and Advocate of Military Professionalism, 1830-71." Ph.D. dissertation, Duke University, 1969.

Griffith, Paddy. *Battle in the Civil War: Generalship and Tactics in America 1861-65.* Nottinghamshire, England: Fieldbooks, 1986.

Griffith, Paddy. "The Battlefield and Its Fortifications." In Paddy Griffith. *Battle Tactics of the Civil War.* New Haven, CT: Yale University Press, 1989, 117-35.

Gross, Gerald G. "Planning Board Seeks Funds for Fort Drive," *The Washington Post*, November. 15, 1940.

Gross, Gerald G. "What's Wrong With the Capital Parks System? Experts Disagree." *The Washington Post*, December 3, 1939.

Guide to the City of Washington, What To See, and How To See It. Washington, DC: Philip & Solomons, 1869. Pages 25-26.

"Guide to the Military Features in and About Washington." In Official Program, Army Relief Society, *Military Exposition and Carnival, War College, Sept. 30th - Oct. 1st, 1927.* Baltimore, MD: Printed by the Monumental Printing Co., 1927(?), 22-40.

"Gun Battery Yields Only Yankee Button," The Evening Star, April 25, 1958.

Gutheim, Frederick. *The Federal City: Plans and Realities.* Washington, D.C.: Smithsonian Institution Press, 1976.

Gutheim, Frederick. *Worthy of the Nation: The History of Planning for the National Capital.* Washington, DC: Smithsonian Institution, 1970.

Hagerman, Edward. "The Evolution of Trench Warfare in the American Civil." Ph.D. dissertation, Duke University, 1965.

Hagerman, Edward. "From Jomini to Dennis Hart Mahan: The Evolution of Trench Warfare and the American Civil War." Civil War History, 13, September 1967, 197-220.

Halle, Guy le. *Histoire des Fortifications de Paris et leur Extension en Ile-de-France.* Lyon, France: Editions Horvath, 1995.

Handly, Jacqui. *Civil War Defenses of Washington, D.C.: A Cultural Landscape Inventory*. Washington, D.C.: The Government Printing Office (Falls Church Office, Denver Service Center, National Park Service), 1996.

Hannum, Warren T. "Water Supply of the District of Columbia." *Professional Memoirs, Corps of Engineers, United States Army and Engineer Department at Large*, 4, March-April 1912, 224-52.

Hansen, Reed. "Civil War to Civil Concern: A History of Fort Marcy, Virginia." M.A. thesis in History, George Mason University, 1973.

Hanson, Joseph Mills. *Bull Run Remembers . . . The History, Traditions and Landmarks of the Manassas (Bull Run) Campaigns Before Washington 1861-1862*. Manassas, VA : National Capitol Publishers, 1961.

Hardin, Martin D. "The Defence of Washington Against Early's Attack in July, 1864." In Military Order of the Loyal Legion of the United States. Illinois Commandery. *Military Essays and Recollections . . .* Volume II. Chicago, IL: A.C. McClure and Company, 1894, 121-44.

Harrington, Peter. *Archaeology of the English Civil War*. Buckinghamshire, England: Shire Publications Ltd., 1992.

Havenner, George C. *Early History of Anacostia or Old Uniontown*. Washington, D.C.: Anacostia Federal Savings & Loan Association, n.d.

Hardin, Martin D. "The Defence of Washington Against Early's Attack in July, 1864." In Military Order of the Loyal Legion of the United States, Illinois Commandery. *Military Essays and Recollections: Papers Read Before the Commandery of the State of Illinois, Military Order of the Loyal Legion of the United States*. Volume II. Chicago, IL: A.C. McClure and company, 1894, 121-

Haskin, Frederic J. "Forts Around Washington." *The Washington Star*, September 8, 1935.

Heitman, Francis B., *Historical Register and Dictionary of the United States Army, from Its Organization, September 29, 1789, to March 2, 1903*. 2 Volumes. Washington, DC: The Government Printing Office, 1903.

Helm, Judith Beck. *Tenleytown, D. C.: Country Village into City Neighborhood*. Washington, DC: Tennally Press, 1981.

Hennessy, John. *The First Battle of Manassas: An End to Innocence July 18-21, 1861*. Lynchburg, VA: H.E. Howard Inc., 1989.

Hennessy, John J. *Return to Bull Run: The Campaign and Battle of Second Manassas.* New York: Simon & Schuster, 1993.

Herron, Leroy W. "Spanish War." Chapter 37. In John Clagett Proctor. Editor. *Washington, Past and Present: A History.* 4 Volumes. New York: Lewis, 1930, 389-97.

Heyden, Neil E. "The Fort Reno Community: The Conversion and Its Causes." Washington, DC: Department of History, American University, 1981.

Hickenlooper, Andrew. "Our Volunteer Engineers." In Ohio Commandery, Military Order of the Loyal Legion of the United States. *Sketches of War History.* Cincinnati, Ohio: Robert Clarke and Company, 1890, 3, 301-18.

Hicks, Frederick C. "Lincoln, Wright, and Holmes at Fort Stevens." *Journal of the Illinois Historical Society,* 39, 1946, 323-32.

Hill, John. *The First Battle of Bull Run: Campaign of First Manassas* (American Civil War Notebook Series). Fairfax, VA: CartoGraphics, Inc., 1991.

Hinds, James R. and Edmund Fitzgerald. "Fortifications in the Field and on the Frontier." *Periodical: The Journal of the Council on America's Military Past,* 9, Spring 1977, 41-48.

Hinds, James R. "Potomac River Defenses: The First Twenty Years." *Periodical: The Journal of the Council on Abandoned Military Posts,* 5, Fall 1973, 2-16.

"Historic Spot Is Site For New Homes," *Washington Times,* Oct 29, 1927.

"History of Fort Drive," In National Capital Planning Commission, *Fort Park System: A Re-Evaluation Study of Fort Drive, Washington, D.C.* April 1965 By Fred W. Tuemmler and Associates, College Park, Maryland. Washington, DC: National Capital Planning Commission, 1965.

The History of Fort Myer Virginia 100th Anniversary Issue (Special Centennial Edition of the fort Myer Post), June 1963.

Hogaland, Kim. *Guide to Resources for Researching Historic Buildings in Washington, D.C.* Revised Edition. Washington, D.C.: N.P., 1962.

Holien, Kim Bernard. *Battle at Ball's Bluff.* Alexandria, VA: The Author, 1985.

Horton, Lois E. "The Days of Jubilee: Black Migration during the Civil War and Reconstruction." In Francine Curro Cary. Editor. *Urban Odyssey: A Multicultural History of Washington, D.C.* Washington, D.C.: Smithsonian Institution Press, 1996, 65-78.

"Housewife's Defiance Saved Fort Marcy," *The Evening Star*, July 29, 1963.

Howard, Oliver Otis. *Autobiography of Oliver Otis Howard Major General United States Army.* Two Volumes. New York: The Baker & Taylor Company, 1908.

Hughes, Maria, "Archaeologists to Probe Fort Marcey Site for Possible Ancient Indian Village Ruins." *Northern Virginia Sun*, Nov 2, 1967.

"Huge Reservoir Is Taking Shape." *The Washington Post and Times Herald*, Thursday, May 10, 1956.

Hughes, James Quentin. *Military Architecture.* Second Edition. Liphook, Hant, England: Beaufort Publishibg Ltd., 1991.

Hume, Gary Leroy. "A Comparative History of Two Early Nineteenth Century Fortifications." M.Arch.Hist., University of Virginia, 1968.

Hunt, Ora Elmer. "Defending the Citadel of the Confederacy (Richmond, VA)." In Francis T. Miller. *The Photographic History of the Civil War.* 10 Volumes. New York: The Review of Reviews Co., 1911, 5, 304-22.

Hunt, Ora Elmer. "Defending the National Capital." In Francis T. Miller. *The Photographic History of the Civil War.* 10 Volumes. New York: The Review of Reviews Co., 1911, 5, 75-108.

Hunt, Ora Elmer. "Engineer Corps of the Federal Army." In Francis T. Miller. *The Photographic History of the Civil War.* 10 Volumes. New York: The Review of Reviews Co., 1911, 5, 222-54.

Hune, Ora Elmer. "Entrenchments and Fortifications." Francis T. Miller. *The Photographic History of the Civil War.* 10 Volumes. New York: The Review of Reviews Co., 1911, 5, 194-218.

Hurd, William B. *Alexandria, Virginia 1861-1865.* Alexandria, VA: City of Alexandria, 1970.

Huston, James A. *The Sinews of War: Army Logistics, 1775-1953.* Washington, DC: The Government Printing Office, 1966.

Hutchins, Stilson and W.F. Morse. *A Souvenir of the Federal Capital and of the National Drill and En-campment at Washington, D.C. May 23d to May 30th, 1887.* Washington, DC: W.F. Morse, 1887.

Hutchinson, Louise Daniel. *The Anacostia Story: 1608-1930* Washington, DC: Published for the Anacostia Neighborhood Museum of the Smithsonian Institution by the Smithsonian Institution Press, 1977.

Hutchinson, Thomas, Andrew Boyd and William H. Boyd. Compilers. *Boyd's Washington and Georgetown Directory* (also known as Hutchinson's Directory, etc.). 10 Volumes. Washington, DC:, 1862-72.

Hyde, John T. *Elementary Principles of Fortification*. London: Wm. H. Allen & Co., 1860.

An Illustrated History: The City of Washington. By the Junior League of Washington. Edited by Thomas Froncek. New York: Alfred A. Knopf, 1979.

"In the Defense of Washington." Appendix I in U. S., Naval History Division. *Civil War Naval Chronology, 1861-1865*. Washington, DC: The Government Printing Office, 1971.

Ingle, Edward. *The Negro in the District of Columbia*. Baltimore, MD: Johns Hopkins University Press, 1893.

Innes, Lieutenant. "Notes on the Defenses of Charleston, South Carolina," In Great Britain, Army, Corps of Royal Engineers. *Papers on Subjects Connected with the Duties of the Royal Engineers . . .* 33 Volumes. Woolwich, England: W.P. Jackson, 1839-76, New Series, 13, 1864, 16-24.

Jacobs, Charles T. *Civil War Guide to Montgomery County, Maryland*. Rockville, MD: The Montgomery County Historical Society and the Montgomery County Civil War Round Table, 1983.

Jacobs, Charles T. *Civil War Guide to Montgomery County, Maryland*. Revised Edition. Rockville, MD: The Montgomery County Historical Society, 1996.

James, Felix. "Freedman's Village, Arlington, Virginia: A History." M.A. thesis, Howard University, 1967.

Jebb, Joshua. *Practical Treatise on Strengthening and Defending Outposts, Villages, Houses, Bridges, &c., in Reference to the Duties of Officers in Command of Picquets, as Laid Down in the Field Exercise and Evolutions of the Army*. Fifth Edition. London: William Clowes and Sons, 1857.

Johnson, Andrews. *The Papers of Andrew Johnson*. Edited by Leroy P. Graf, Ralph W. Haskins and Paul H. Bergeron. Multivolume. Knoxville, TN: University of Tennessee Press, 1967-.

Johnson, Leland R. "Civil War Railroad Defenses." *Tennessee Valley Historical Review*, 2, Summer 1972, 20-26.

Johnson, Ludwell H. "Civil War Military History: A Few Revisions in Need of Revising." *Civil War History*, 17, June 1971, 115-130.

Johnson, W.C. and E.S. Hartshorn. "The Development of Field Fortifications in the Civil War." *Professional Memoirs, Corps of Engineers, United States Army and Engineer Department at Large*, 7, September October 1915, 570-602.

Johnston, Allen John. "Surviving Freedom": The Black Community of Washington, D.C., 1860-1870. Ph.D. dissertation, Duke University, 1880.

Johnston, Charles. "Attack on Fort Gilmer." *Southern Historical Society Papers*, 1, June 1876, 438-42 (Petersburg).

Johnston, R.M.. *Bull Run: Its Strategy and Tactics*. New York: Houghton Mifflin, 1913.

Jones, Dr. "Washington, July 10, 1864." *Southern Historical Society Papers*, 22 1894, 298-299.

Jones, Archer. "Jomini and the Strategy of the American Civil War, A Reinterpretation." *Military Affairs*, 34, December 1970, 127-31.

Jones, Jesse H. and George S. Greene. "The Breastworks at Culp's Hill." In *Battles and Leaders of the Civil War* . . . Edited by Robert U. Johnson and Clarence C. Buell. 4 Volumes. New York: The Century Company, 1887-88, III, 316-17.

Jones, Virgil C. "Action Along the Union Outposts in Fairfax." Historical Society of Fairfax County, Virginia, Inc. *Yearbook*, 3, 1954, 1-3.

Jones, Virgil C. "First Manassas: The Story of the Bull Run Campaign." *Civil War Times Illustrated*, 19, No. 4, 1980, 3-12, 16-45.

Jordan, Philip D. "The Capital of Crime." *Civil War Times Illustrated*, 13, February 1975, 4-9, 44-47.

"Jubal Early's Raid on Washington." In Noah Brooks. *Mr. Lincoln's Washington: Selections from the Writings of Noah Brooks Civil War Correspondent*. Edited by P.J. Staudenraus. New York: Thomas Yoseloff, 1967, 352-56.

Judge, Joseph. *Season of Fire: The Confederate Strike on Washington*. Berryville, VA: Rockbridge Publishing Company, 1994.

Julian, Allen P. "Atlanta's Defenses: The Fortifications Protecting Atlanta." *Civil War Times Illustrated*, 3, July 1964, 23-24.

Keckley, Elizabeth. *Behind the Scenes: Life of A Colored Woman Thirty Years A Slave, Four Years at the White House*. Reprint of 1931 Edition. New York: Arno Press, 1968.

Keim, Randolph. *Keim's Illustrated Hand-Book. Washington and Its Environs: A Descriptive and Historical Hand-Book to the Capital of the United States of America* Fourth Edition, corrected to July, 1874 (Washington, DC: For the Compiler, 1874.

Kelly, Dennis. "The Second Battle of Manassas." *Civil War Times Illustrated*, 22, No. 3, 1983, 8-44.

Kelly, Kathleen Anne. "Fortification of Washington, DC During the Civil War: Implications and Realities." M. A. Thesis in Architectural History, University of Virginia, 1984.

Kelso, Jack. "Court Stalls Route 66 For Union Fortification." *The Washington Star*, November 30, 1960.

Kennedy, Will P. "Linking of Forts Embodied in Plan." *The Washington Star*, December 4, 1925.

Kimmel, Stanley. *Mr. Lincoln's Washington*. New York: Coward-McCann, Inc., 1957.

Kindmark, Robert G. "John Gross Barnard: His Civil War Career and Military Writings." Unpublished manuscript submitted for course, History 50, Allegheny College, Meadville, PA, April 30, 1978.

Kleber, Louis C. "August, 1862: The Second Battle of Bull Run." *History Today*, 28, No. 12, 1978, 803-09.

Kline, Jerry, "Alexandria Restores Old Civil War Fort," *The Washington Star*, Aug 5, 1962.

Kneitel, Tom. *Directory of U.S. Army Forts, Camps, & Airfields (1789-1945*. Commack, NY: CRB Research Books, Inc., 1992.

Kohler, Sue A. *The Commission of Fine Arts: A Brief History: 1910-1990*. Washington, DC: Commission on Fine Arts, 1991.

Kohn, Bernard. "Restored Civil War Fort Is New Sightseeing Shrine," *The Sunday Washington Star*, July 4, 1937.

Krick, Robert K. "Fire and Stone." In *Touched by Fire: A Photographic Portrait of the Civil War*. Edited by William C. Davis. Boston: Little, Brown and Company, 1986, Volume 2, 111-58.

Lackey, Louana M. "A Preliminary Archaeological and Historical Survey of A Portion of Fort Reno Park in Washington, D. C. Prepared by the Department of General Services of the District of Columbia." Washington, DC: The Potomac River Archeology Survey, American University, 1983.

"Langdon Resigns, Criticizing Post." *The Washington Star*, May 2, 1926.

Lee, Richard M. *General Lee's City: An Illustrated Guide to the Historic Sites of Confederate Richmond.* McLean, VA: EPM Publications, Inc., 1987.

Lee, Richard M. *Mr. Lincoln's City: An Illustrated Guide to the Civil War Sites of Washington.* McLean, VA: EPM Publications, Inc., 1981.

Leech, Margaret. *Reveille in Washington.* New York: Harper & Brothers Publishers, 1941.

"Legislative History of the Office of National Capital Parks." Compiled in the National Capital Parks Office, July, 1940.

Lendy, Auguste Frederic. *Elements of Fortification, Field and Permanent.* London: John W. Parker and Son, 1857.

Lendy, Augustus Frederic. *Treatise on Fortification. Or, Lectures Delivered to Officers Reading for the Staff.* London: W. Mitchell, 1862.

Lessoff, Alan H. *The Federal Government and the National Capital--Washington, 1861-1902.* Thesis, Johns Hopkins Univ, 1990.

Lewis, Emanuel Raymond. *Seacoast Fortifications of the United States: An Introductory History.* Washington, DC: Smithsonian Institution Press, 1970.

Lilley, David A. "Mapping in North America, 1775 to 1865, Emphasizing Union Military Topography in the Civil War." M.A. Thesis, George Mason University, 1982.

Lincoln Day by Day: A Chronology, 1809-1865. Volume III: 1861-1865. Washington, DC: The Government Printing Office, 1960.

"Linking of Forts Embodied in Plan," *The Washington Star*, December 4, 1925

Lippitt, Francis J. *A Treatise on Intrenchments.* New York: D. Van Nostrand, Publisher, 1866.

Lissimore, John Troy C. "Defenses of Washington, 1861-1865." M.A. thesis, Howard University, 1971.

Little, Glenn J., II. *Archaeological Research—Fort Earthworks: Fort Davis, Fort Mahan, Fort Dupont, for the National Park Service.* Division of Archaeology, Department of the Interior, 1968.

Longyear, John Munro. "Georgetown during the Civil War." *Georgetown Today*, 7, March 1975, 6-10.

Look to the Earth: Historical Archaeology and the American Civil War. Edited by Clarence R. Geier, Jr. and Susan E. Winter. Knoxville, TN: University of Tennessee Press, 1994.

Lord, Francis A. "Army and Navy Textbooks and Manuals Used by the North during the Civil War." *Military Collector & Historian*, 9, Fall 1957, 61-67; Winter 1957, 95-102.

Lounsbury, Thomas H. "In the Defenses of Washington." *Yale Review*, 2, April 1913, 385-411.

Lowry, Don. *Fate of the Country: The Civil War From June to September 1864*. NY: Hippocrene, 1992.

Luvaas, Jay. "Introduction." In *The U.S. Army War College Guide to the Battles of Chancellorsville & Fredericksburg*. Edited by Dr. Jay Luvaas and Col. Harold W. Nelson. Carlisle, PA: South Mountain Press, Inc., 1988, x-xiv.

Luvaas, Jay. *The Military Legacy of the Civil War: The European Inheritance*. Chicago: The University of Chicago Press, 1959.

Lykes, Richard W. *Campaign for Petersburg*. Washington, DC: The Government Printing Office, 1970.

Lykes, Richard W. *Petersburg Battlefields*. Washington, DC: The Government Printing Office, 1951.

McClellan, George B. *McClellan's Own Story. The War for the Union, the Soldiers Who Fought It, the Civilians Who Directed It And His Relations to It and to Them*. New York: Charles L. Webster & Company, 1887.

McClure, Stanley W. *Guide Leaflets for the Tour of Historic Civil War Defenses, Washington, D.C.* Washington, DC: The National Park Service, 1938.

McDonough, M.J. and P.S. Bond. "Use and Development of the Ponton Equipage in the United States Army with Special Reference to the Civil War." *Professional Memoirs, Corps of Engineers, United States Army and Engineer Department at Large*, 6, November-December 1914, 692-758.

McElroy, John. Editor. "The Civil War." Chapter 36. In John Clagett Proctor. Editor. *Washington, Past and Present: A History*. 4 Volumes. New York: Lewis, 1930, 376-88.

McElwee, William. *The Art of War: Waterloo to Mons*. Bloomington, IN: Indiana University Press, 1974.

McFall, Lawrence. *The Fortifications of Danville, Virginia During the War Between the States 1861-1865*. Danville, VA: N.P., 1984.

McCormick, Charles H. *General Background: Forts Mahan, Chaplin, Dupont, Davis.* Washington, DC: Division of History, Office of Archeology and Historic Preservation, National Park Service, 1967.

McWhiney, Grady. "Who Whipped Whom? Confederate Defeat Reexamined." *Civil War History*, 11, March 1956, 5-26.

McWhiney, Grady and Perry D. Jamieson. *Attack and Die: Civil War Military Tactics and the Southern Heritage.* University, AL: The University of Alabama Press, 1982.

Macaulay, J.S. *A Treatise on Field Fortification and Other Subjects Connected with the Duties of the Field Engineer.* London: James Fraser, 1834.

Mackintosh, Barry. *Rock Creek Park: An Administrative History.* Washington, DC: National Park Service, 1985.

Macqueen, Philip 0. "New Aqueduct for the National Capital." *The Military Engineer*, 18, March-April 1926, 110-17.

Macqueen, Philip 0. "Cabin John Bridge." *The Military Engineer*, 24, November- December 1932, 566-68.

Macqueen, Philip 0. "Repairing Old Water-supply Conduit." *The Military Engineer*, 19, September-October 1927, 410-11.

Macqueen, Philip 0. "Rock Creek Bridge." *The Military Engineer*, 28, March April 193₆. 111-13.

Magnusson, Jan. "Fort Scott." *The Arlington Historical Magazine*, 2, October 1964, 37-47.

Mahan, Dennis Hart. *A Complete Treatise on Field Fortification, with the General Outlines of the Principles Regulating the Arrangement, the Attack, and the Defense of Permanent Works.* New York: Wiley & Long, 1836.

Mahan, Dennis Hart. *Summary of the Course of Permanent Fortification and of the Attack and Defence of Permanent Works, for the Use of the Cadets of the U.S. Military Academy.* Richmond, VA: West and Johnston, 1863.

Mahan, Dennis Hart. *A Treatise on Field Fortification, Containing Instructions on the Method of Laying Out, Constructing, Defending, and Attacking Intrenchments, With the General Outlines Also of the Arrangement, the Attack, and Defence of Permanent Fortifications.* Third Edition, Revised and Enlarged. New York: John Wiley, 1861.

Mahon, John K. "Civil War Infantry Assault Tactics." *Military Affairs*, 25, Summer 1961, 57-68.

"Marking the Forts" *The Washington Star, Sunday Magazine*, September 11, 1966.

Mears, David. "A View of Washington in 1863." *Records of the Columbia Historical Society of Washington, D.C.*, 1963-65, 210-20.

Melder, Keith E. "Angel of Mercy in Washington: Josephine Griffing and the Freedmen, 1864-1872." *Records of the Columbia Historical Society of Washington, D.C.*, Vols. 63-65, 1966, 243-72.

Meglis, Anne Llewellyn. Compiler. *A Bibliographic Tour of Washington, DC.* Washington, DC: D.C. Redevelopment Land Agency, 1974.

Merrill, William E. "Block-houses for the Railroad Defense in the Department of the Cumberland." In Military Order of the Loyal Legion of the United States, Ohio Commandery. *Sketches of War History, 1861-1865.* Cincinnati, Ohio: Robert Clarke and Company, 1890, 3, 384-421.

Merrill, William E. "Blockhouses--Federal Means of Protecting Communication." *Civil War Times Illustrated*, 4, January 1966, 34-39.

Merrill, William E. "The Engineer Service in the Army of the Cumberland." In Thomas B. Van Horne. *History of the Army of the Cumberland* . . . Cincinnati, Ohio: Robert Clarke and Company, 1875, 2, 439-58.

Merrill, William E. "Map Reproduction." *Professional Memoirs, Corps of Engineers, United States Army and Engineer Department at Large*, 1, October-December 1909, 414-16.

Meyer, Eugene L. "Holding Down the Fort in D.C." *The Washington Post*, Friday, January 23, 1987.

Miller, Alexander M. *Water Supply of Washington, D. C., Engineer School Occasional Paper No. 15.* Washington, DC: Engineer School, 1904.

Miller, David V. *The Defense of Washington During the Civil War.* Buffalo, New York: Mr. Copy, 1976.

Military Historical Society of Massachusetts, Boston. *The Virginia Campaign of 1862.* New York: Published for the Society by Houghton Mifflin, 1895.

Miller, Francis T. *The Photographic History of the Civil War.* Ten Volumes. New York: The Review of Reviews Co., 1911.

Miller, John, Jr. "Men, Weapons and Tactics." *Army Information Digest*, 16, August 1961, 47-51.

Miller, T. Michael. "Jones Point: Haven of History." The Historical Society of Fairfax County, Virginia *Yearbook*, Volume 21— 1986-1988, 15-73.

Miller, T. Michael. "The Saga of Shuter's Hill (Fort Ellsworth)." *The Historical Society of Fairfax County, Virginia*, Volume 19, 1983, 74-113.

Miller, William J. *The Men of Fort Ward: Defenders of Washington*. Alexandria, VA: The Friends of Fort Ward, 1989.

Mitchell, Mary. *Divided Town: A Study of Georgetown, D.C. During the Civil War*. Barre, MA: Barre Publishers, 1968.

Mitchell, William A. *Army Engineering*. Washington, DC: The Society of American Military Engineers, 1927.

Mitchell, William A. *Fortification*. Washington, DC: The Society of American Military Engineers, 1927.

"Modern Shopping Center Stands Near Civil War Shooting Grounds," *The Washington Daily News*, October 3, 1956;

Morgan, James Dudley. *Historic Fort Washington*. Washington, DC: N.P. 1904.

Morgan, James Dudley. "Historic Fort Washington on the Potomac." *Records of the Columbia Historical Society of Washington, D.C*, 7, 1904, 1-19.

Mosley, Thomas V. "Evolution of American Civil War Infantry Tactics." Ph.D. dissertation, University of North Carolina, 1967.

Moulton, Charles H. *Fort Lyon To Harper's Ferry: On the Border of North and South with "Rambling Tour"*. *The Letters and Newspaper Dispatches of Charles H. Moulton (34th Mass Vol. Inf.)*. Compiled and Edited by Lee C. Drickamer and Karen D. Drickamer. Shippensburg, PA: White Mane Publishing Co., Inc., 1987.

"Move To Preserve Forts As D.C. Parks." *The Washington Star*, January 24, 1926.

Muller, Charles G. "Fabulous Potomac Passage." *U.S. Naval Institute Proceedings*, 90, May 1964, 85-91.

Munden, Kenneth W. and Henry Putney Beers. *Guide to Federal Archives Relating to the Civil War*. Washington, DC: The Government Printing Office, 1962.

Munsey, Everard. "Capital's Citadel of 1861 Being Restored as Park," *The Washington Post*, July 15, 1961.

Myer, Donald B. *Bridges and the City of Washington*. Wash, DC: The Government Printing Office, 1974.

A Narrative History of Fort Myer Virginia. Litho-Print Press, Falls Church, VA, 1954(?).

"National Capital Park and Planning Commission." In H.S. Wagner and Charles G. Sauers. *Study of the Organization of the National Capital Parks*. Washington, DC: The National Park Service, National Capital Parks, 1939, 39-41.

National Military Park to Commemorate Battle of Fort Stevens. Hearings Before the Committee on Military Affairs, House of Representatives, Sixty-Eighth Congress, Second Session, on H.R. 11365, Monday, January 12, 1925, Statement of Hon. Samuel E. Cook of Indiana. Washington, DC: The Government Printing Office, 1925.

Neary, John, "Bearded Bus Dweller Probes Fort's Ruins," *The Washington Star*, June 36, 1961.

Nesbitt, Mark. *Rebel Rivers: A Guide to Civil War Sites on the Potomac, Rappahannock, York, and James*. Mechanicsburg, PA: Stackpole Books, 1993.

Ness, George T., Jr. "Army Engineers of the Civil War." *The Military Engineer*, 57, January-February 1965, 38-40.

Ness, George T. "Engineers of the Civil War." *The Military Engineer*, 44, May-June 1952, 179-87.

Nettesheim, Daniel D. "Topographical Intelligence and the American Civil War." Unpublished Masters thesis, U.S. Army Command and General Staff College, 1978.

Newell, Frederick Haynes. Editor. *Planning and Building the City of Washington*. Published by the Washington Society of Engineers. Washington, DC: Ransdell, Inc., 1932.

Nichols, James L. *Confederate Engineers*. Tuscaloosa, AL: Confederate Publishing Company, Inc., 1957.

O'Brien, William J. "The Washington Arsenal, Historic Landmark of the Nation's Capital." *Army Ordnance*, 16, July-August 1935, 32-37.

"Old Fort Stevens Sold, Purchased by Syndicate of Virginia and Maryland Capitalists": *The Washington Star*, March 22, 1911.

"Old Forts in Capital Park System." *The Washington Star*, August 3, 1933.

"Old Gun Emplacement Halts School Bulldozer, " *The Washington Star*, Apr 23, 1958.

Oliver, Thomas, "Ft. Ward Emerges in Changed Role," *The Washington Star*, June 26, 1967.

Olmsted, Frederick Law, Jr. "Border Roads for Parkways and Parks." *Landscape Architecture, 16* 1925, 74-84.

Olszewski, George J. *Historic Structures Report: Forts Carroll and Greble, Washington, D.C.* Washington, DC: Office of History and Historic Architecture, Eastern Service Center, National Park Service, 1970.

Oman, Anne H. "The Forts of Washington: Only Two Saw Hostile Action." *The Washington Post*, Weekend, May 27, 1983..

"1,080,000 Asked for Fort Drive." *The Washington Star*, August 24, 1938.
Osborne, Charles C. "Early's Raid on Washington." *MHQ: The Quarterly Journal of Military History*, 6, Autumn 1993, 100-109.

"Our Capital in Wartimes." Chapter IV. In *Washington: Yesterday and Today*. Prepared by Social Studies Teachers in the Washington, D.C., Public Schools under the direction of George J. Jones. Boston, MA: Ginn and Company, 1943, 54-72.

Owen, Thomas J. *"Dear Friends at Home . . .": The Letters and Diary of Thomas James Owen, Fiftieth New York Volunteer Engineer Regiment, During the Civil War*. Edited with an Introduction by Dale E. Floyd. Washington, DC: The Government Printing Office, 1985.

"Palisades, Forts, and Wars." In Frederick Tilp. *This Was the Potomac River*. Alexandria, VA: Published by the Author, 1978, 164-82.

"Park Board Approves Changes In Fort Drive Project Plans." *The Washington Post*, June 21, 1947.

"Park Board May Wreck Historic Fort," *The Washington Post*, October 28, 1937;

Parkway to Connect Forts in District of Columbia, House Report No. 649, 67th Congress, 2d Session, February 3, 1923.

Parkway Connecting Civil War Forts, Calendar No. 627, *Senate Report No. 585*, 68th Congress, 1st Session, May 20, 1924, May 20 (calendar day, May 22), 1924.

"The Past, Present and Future of Fortifications." *Army & Navy Journal*, I, December 26, 1863, 276.

Penfield, Alanson. *A Tale of the Rebellion: Facts and Figures from the Standpoint of A Departmental Clerk*. 2nd Edition. Washington, DC: Intelligence Printing House, 1867.

Piron, F.P.J. "The Systems of Fortification Discussed and Compared." *United States Service Magazine*, 5, January 1866, 34-40; February 1866, 108-14; March 1866, 225-34; April 1866, 328-32.

Poe, Orlando M. "The Defense of Knoxville." In *Battles and Leaders of the Civil War* . . . Edited by Robert U. Johnson and Clarence C. Buell. 4 Volumes. New York: The Century Company, 1887-88, III, 731-45.

Poe, Orlando M., et al. "The Engineers with General Sherman's Army." *Professional Memoirs, Corps of Engineers, United States Army and Engineer Department at Large*, 6, May-June 1914, 358-94.

"The Present Condition of the Defenses of Washington, Built during the Civil War, 1861-1865." In Frank L. Averill. *Guide to the National Capital and Maps of Vicinity including the Fortifications*. Washington, DC: Published by The Engineering Platoon of the Engineer Corps, D.C.N.G. , 1892, 14-24.

Price, William H. "Civil War Military Operations in Northern Virginia in May-June 1861." *The Arlington Historical Magazine*, 2, October 1961, 43-49, 57.

Proctor, John Clagett. "The Battle of Fort Stevens: Early's Invasion of Washington July 11, 12, 1864." In John Clagett Proctor. *Proctor's Washington and Environs, Written for the Washington Sunday Star (1928-1949)*. Washington, DC: Published by the Author, 1949, 347-51.

Proctor, John Clagett., ed. *Washington, Past and Present: A History.* 4 Volumes. New York: Lewis, 1930.

Public Park at Fort Thayer, District of Columbia, Senate Report No. 362, 60th Cong., 1st Sess., Washington, DC: The Government Printing Office, 1908.

R. Christopher Goodwin and Associates. *Historic Resources Survey: Addendum to the 1970 Historic Structures Report—Forts Carroll and Greble*. Washington, DC: National Park Service, 1991.

Raines, Rebecca Robbins . *"Getting the Message Through": A Branch History of the U.S. Army Signal Corps Army Historical Series*. Washington, DC: The Government Printing Office, 1996.

The Rambler (Richard Rogers), "Old Fort Resists Siege of Time," *The Washington Star*, October 19, 1956.

Reps, John W. *Monumental Washington: The Planning and Development of the Capital Center*. Princeton, NJ: Princeton University Press, 1967.

Richards, David Allen. "Civil War Diary of David Allen Richards." Edited with an Introduction by Frederick D. Williams. *Michigan History*, 39, June 1955, 183-220.

"A Ring of Parks." *The Washington Post*, May 14, 1965.

Risch, Erna. *Quartermaster Support of the Army: A History of the Corps, 1775-1939.* Washington, DC: The Government Printing Office, 1962.

Roberts, Chalmers M. *Washington, Past and Present: A Pictorial History of the Nation's Capital.* Washington, DC: Public Affairs Press, 1950.

Roberts, Robert B. *Encyclopedia of Historic Forts: The Military, Pioneer, and Trading Posts of the United States.* New York: Macmillan Publishing Company, 1988.

Robertson, W. Glenn. "First Bull Run, 19 July 1861." Chapter 4 in *America's First Battles 1776-1965.* Edited by Charles E. Heller and William A. Stofft. Lawrence, KS: University Press of Kansas, 1986, 81-108.

Robertson, James I., Jr. *Civil War Sites in Virginia: A Tour Guide.* Charlottesville, VA: The University Press of Virginia, 1982.

Robertson, James I., Jr. *Civil War Virginia: Battleground for a Nation.* Charlottesville, VA: The University Press of Virginia, 1991.

Robinson, Henry S. "Some Aspects of the Free Negro Population of Washington, D.C., 1860-1862." *Maryland Historical Magazine,* 64, Spring 1969, 43-64.

Robinson, Willard B. *American Forts: Architectural Form and Function.* Urbana, IL: University of Illinois Press, 1977.

Robinson, Willard B. "Maritime Frontier Engineering: The Defense of New Orleans." *Louisiana History,* 18, Winter 1977, 5-62.

Rose, Cornelia B., Jr. "Civil War Forts in Arlington." *Arlington (Virginia) Historical Magazine,* 1, October 1960, 14-27.

Rose, Cornelia B., Jr. "Civil War Forts in Arlington." *Northern Virginia Sun,* March 14, 1960.

Royall, R.E. "The Mount Vernon Memorial Highway." *The Military Engineer,* 24, May- June 1932, 238-42.

Ryan, Jim. "History Afoot At the Forts." *The Washington Post,* Weekend, January 6, 1989.

Sadler, Christine. "One More Mile and the District Will Have a Driveway Linking Forts, Road to Pass Fortifications of Civil War, Will Run Along Rims of Hills That Make Saucer of City, Expected to Be One of Nation's Most Scenic and Historic," *The Washington Post,* Sunday, October 10, 1937.

Salamanca, Lucy. "When Washington Was Fort Girdled." *Washington Post,* January 25, 1931, pages 5 , 17.

Salay, David L. "Everyday Life at Fort Washington, Maryland, 1861-1872." *Maryland Historical Magazine*, 87, Winter 1992, 420-27.

Salay, David L. "'very picturesque, but regarded as nearly useless': Fort Washington, Maryland, 1816-1872." *Maryland Historical Magazine*, 81, Spring 1986, 67-86.

Schauffelen, Otmar. *Die Bundesfestung und ihre Geschichte europas groBte Festungsanlage.* Ulm, Germany: Armin Vaas Verlag, 1989.

Scheips, Paul J. "'Old Probabilities': A.J. Myer and the Signal Corps Weather Service." *The Arlington Historical Magazine*, 5, October 1974, 29-43.

Schildt, Bobbi. "Freedman's Village." *Northern Virginia Heritage*, 7, February 1985, 10-14, 19-20.

Schmitt, Edwin A. and Philip 0. Macqueen. "Washington Aqueduct." *The Military Engineer*, 41, May-June 1949, 205-10.

Schumann, Paul. "Fort Negley: Guardian of Nashville." *Periodical: The Journal of the Council on Abandoned Military Posts*, 12, January 1981, 24-35.

Scott, Henry L. *Military Dictionary: Comprising Technical Definitions; Information on Raising and Keeping Troops; Actual Service Including Makeshifts and Improved Material; and Law, Government, Regulation, and Administration Relating to Land Forces.* New York: D. Van Nostrand, 1861.

Sedgwick, Paul J. *The Shield.* Washington, DC: The District of Columbia Civil War Centennial Commission, 1965.

"Semipermament Defenses." In U.S., Engineer School. *Pamphlet on the Evolution of the Art of Fortification, Engineer School Occasional Paper No. 58.* Prepared Under the Direction of William M. Black. Washington, DC: The Government Printing Office, 1919, 87-90.

Seymour, Digby Gordon. *Divided Loyalties; Fort Sanders and the Civil War in East Tennessee.* Knoxville, TN: University of Tennessee Press, 1963.

Shaheen, Chris. "The Fort Drive: The Influence and Adaptation of A 20th Century Planning Effort in Washington, D.C. Paper in George Washington University Historic Preservation Course (Professor Richard Longstreth), May 30, 1994.

Shannon, J. Harby. *Index to "The Rambler" A Series of Articles by J. Harby Shannon on Washington and vicinity Published in The Sunday Star, Washington, D.C. over A Period of Years between 1912-1927.*

Reprinted from the *Records of Columbia Historical Society of Washington, D.C.*, Fiftieth Anniversary Volume 46-47. Washington, DC: Columbia Historical Society, 1947.

Shea, William L. "The Camden Fortifications." *Arkansas Historical Quarterly*, 41, Winter 1982, 318-26.

Shiman, Philip Lewis. "Engineering Sherman's March: Army Engineers and the Management of Modern War, 1862-1865." Ph.D. dissertation, Duke University, 1991.

Shosteck, Robert. *25 Hikes in and Near Washington.* Washington, DC: Capital Transit Company, 1946.

Shoup, Francis A. "Dalton Campaign--Works at Chattahoochee--Inteeresting History." *Confederate Veteran*, 3, September 1895, 262-65.

"Site of 7 Corners Center Once Called fort Buffalo," *The Washington Post*, Oct. 3, 1956

Smelser, Marshall. "Naval Considerations in the Location of the National Capital." *Maryland Historical Magazine*, March 1957, 72-74.

Smith, Howard K., *Washington, D.C.: The Study of Our Nations Capital.* New York: Random House, Inc., 1967.

Smith, Katheryn Schneider. Editor. *Washington at Home: An Illustrated History of Neighborhoods in the Nation's Capital.* Northridge, CA: Windsor Publications, 1988.

Smith, Samuel D., Fred M. Prouty and Benjamin C. Nance. *A Survey of Civil War Period Military Sites in Middle Tennessee, Tennessee Department of Conservation, Division of Archaeology, Report of Investigations No. 7.* Nashville, TN: Division of Archaeology, Tennessee Department of Conservation, 1990.

Snell, T. Loftin. *The Stranger's Guide to Washington, D.C.* (with map of the city) Washington, DC: Published by the Author, 1967.

Soderberg, Susan Cooke. *Lest We Forget: A Guide to Civil War Monuments in Maryland.* Shippensburg, PA: White Mane Publishing Company, Inc., 1995.

"Some Forts of the Civil War." In Daughters of the American Revolution, District of Columbia, State Historic Committee. *Historical Directory of the District of Columbia.* Washington, DC: State Historic Committee, District of Columbia, Daughters of the American Revolution, 1922, 74.

Sommers, Richard J. *Richmond Redeemed: The Siege at Petersburg.* Garden City, NY: Doubleday & Company, Inc., 1981.

Spier, William. *A History of the Ninth and Tenth Regiments, Rhode Island Volunteers*. Providence, RI: Snow and Farnham, 1872.

Stackpole, Edward James. *From Cedar Mountain to Antietam, August-September, 1862: Cedar Mountain, Second Manassas, Chantilly, Harpers Ferry, South Mountain, Antietam*. Harrisburg, PA: Stackpole, Company, 1959.

Stepp, John W. And William I. Hill. Editors. *Mirror of War*. Englewood Cliffs, NJ: Prentiss Hall, 1961.

Stewart, John. "Early Maps and Surveyors of the City of Washington, D. C." *Records of the Columbia Historical Society of Washington, D. C.*, 2, 1899, 48-71.

Stone, Charles P. "Washington in March and April, 1861." *Magazine of American History* 14 1885, 1-24.

Straith, Hector. *Treatise on Fortification and Artillery*. London, England: Waller & Co., 1850.

Strayer, Martha. "JFK Settles Battle Over Ft. Drive," *Washington Daily News*, May 28, 1963.

Strayer, Martha. "Old Fort Foote, A Forlorn and Forgotten Place." *The Washington Daily News*, Monday, July 20, 1931.

Stuntz, Connie P., & Mayo S. *This Was Tysons Corner, Virginia: Facts and Photos*. Vienna, VA: By the Authors, 1990.

Stuntz, Connie P., & Mayo S. *This Was Vienna, Virginia: Facts and Photos*. Vienna, VA: By the Authors, 1987.

Sullivan, Barry. "Boulevard Is Proposed to Link Capital with Old Fort Washington (New Drive to Encircle City, Link Fortresses)." *The Washington Post*, Sunday, February 6, 1938.

(Sydenham) Clarke, George S. *Fortification: Its Past Achievements, Recent Developments, and Future Progress*. London, England: J. Murray, 1890.

Sydenham, George S. Clarke. "Provisional Fortification." Paper XIII. *Professional Papers of the Corps of Royal Engineers. Royal Engineers Institute Occasional Papers*, III (1879), 253-56 & plate.

"Systems of Fortifications." *Army & Navy Journal*, I, January 2, 1864, 293.

Talley, J. Wallace. *Jamboree Time in Washington*. Washington, DC: 1936.

Tames, Mike. "The Civil War in Northwest Washington." In *Origins II*. Washington, DC: Neighborhood Planning Council #2 and #3, 1976, 17-21.

Templeman Eleanor Lee. "Fort Marcy's Fate Uncertain" (Fairfax Heritage No. 3). *Northern Virginia Sun*, February 28, 1958.

Thatcher, Joseph M. "Chevaux-de-frise: Hardware and Construction." *Military Collector & Historian*, 38, Winter 1986, 169-72.

Thienel, Phillip M. "Engineers in the Union Army, 1861-1865." *The Military Engineer*, 47, January-February 1955, 36-41; March-April 1955, 110-15.

Thompson, Gilbert. *The Engineer Battalion in the Civil War: A Contribution to the History of the United States Engineers, Engineer School Occasional Paper No. 44*. Washington, DC: Press of the Engineer School, 1910.

Tindall, William. *Standard History of the City of Washington, From a Study of the Original Sources*. Knoxville, TN: H.W. Crew and Company, 1914.

Tooley, Mark. "Battle at Fort Stevens Saved." *The Washington Post*, August 6, 1994.

Toomey, Daniel Carroll. *The Civil War in Maryland*. Baltimore, MD: Toomey Press, 1983 (sixth edition, 1993).

Townsend, George Alfred. *Washington, Outside and Inside. A Picture and A Narrative of the Origin, Growth, Excellences, Abuses, Beauties, and Personages of Our Governing City*. James Betts & Co., 1873.

Toy, Sidney. *A History of Fortification from 3000 B.C. to A.D. 1700*. London, England: Heinemann, 1955.

Turtle, Thomas. "History of the Engineer Battalion." *Printed Papers of the Essay on Club of the Corps of Engineers*. Willet's Point, NY: Battalion Press, 1872, I, No. 8.

"Uncle Sam Offers Fine Residence For $80 a Month." *The Washington Post*, December 27, 1940.

Union Calendar No. 520, H.R. 11365, (*House Report No. 1537*), 68th Congress, 2D Session, February 20, 1925.

United States Statutes at Large, Containing the Laws and Concurrent Resolutions . . . and Reorganization Plans, Amendments to the Constitution and Proclamations, 1789-. Washington, D.C.: The Government Printing Office, 1845-.

U. S., Adjutant General's Office, *List of Military Posts, etc.*. Washington, DC: The Government Printing Office, 1902.

U.S., Armed Forces Information School, Carlisle Barracks, Pennsylvania, *The Army Almanac: A Book of Facts Concerning the Army of the United States*. Washington, DC: The Government Printing Office, 1950.

U.S., Army, Corps of Engineers. *Annual Report of the Chief of Engineers to the Secretary of War for the Year 1870. Washington*, DC: The Government Printing Office, 1870.

U.S., Army, Corps of Engineers. *Annual Report of the Chief of Engineers to the Secretary of War for the Year 1873, House Executive Document 1*, Part 2, Vol. II. Washington, DC: The Government Printing Office, 1873.

U.S., Army, Corps of Engineers. *Annual Report of the Chief of Engineers to the Secretary of War for the Year 1874, House Executive Document 1*, Part 2, Vol. II. Washington, DC: The Government Printing Office, 1874.

U.S., Army, Corps of Engineers. *Annual Report of the Chief of Engineers to the Secretary of War for the Year 1875, House Executive Document 1*, Part 2, Vol. II. Washington, DC: The Government Printing Office, 1875.

U.S., Army, Corps of Engineers. *Annual Report of the Chief of Engineers to the Secretary of War for the Year 1876, House Executive Document 1*, Part 2, Vol. II. Washington, DC: The Government Printing Office, 1876.

U.S., Army, Corps of Engineers. *Annual Report of the Chief of Engineers to the Secretary of War for the Year 1877, House Executive Document 1*, Part 2, Vol. II. Washington, DC: The Government Printing Office, 1877.

U.S., Army, Corps of Engineers. *Annual Report of the Chief of Engineers to the Secretary of War for the Year 1878, House Executive Document 1*, Part 2, Vol. II. Washington, DC: The Government Printing Office, 1878.

U.S., Army, Corps of Engineers. *Annual Report of the Chief of Engineers to the Secretary of War for the Year 1879, House Executive Document 1*, Part 2, Vol. II. Washington, DC: The Government Printing Office, 1879.

U.S., Army, Corps of Engineers. *Annual Report of the Chief of Engineers to the Secretary of War for the Year 1880, House Executive Document 1*, Part 2, Vol. II. Washington, DC: The Government Printing Office, 1880.

U.S., Army, Corps of Engineers. *Annual Report of the Chief of Engineers to the Secretary of War for the Year 1882, House Executive Document 1*, Part 2, Vol. II. Washington, DC: The Government Printing Office, 1882.

U.S., Army, Corps of Engineers. *Annual Report of the Chief of Engineers, United States Army, to the Secretary of War for the Year 1885, House Executive Document 1*, Part 2, Vol. II. Washington, DC: The Government Printing Office, 1885.

U.S., Army, Corps of Engineers. *History of the Washington Aqueduct.* Written by Philip O. Macqueen. Washington, DC: Washington District, Corps of Engineers, 1953.

U.S., Army, Corps of Engineers. *Report of the Chief of Engineers Accompanying Report of Secretary of War, 1867.* Washington, DC: The Government Printing Office, 1870.

U. S., Army, Judge Advocate General. *Military Reservations, and Military Parks, and National Cemeteries* Compiled by James B. McCrellis. Washington, DC: The Government Printing Office, 1898.

U. S., Army, Judge Advocate General. *United States Military Reservations, National Cemeteries, and Military Parks* Edited by Charles E. Hay, Jr. Washington, DC: The Government Printing Office, 1904.

U. S., Army, Judge Advocate General. *United States Military Reservations, National Cemeteries, and Military Parks* Edited by Lewis W. Call. Washington, DC: The Government Printing Office, 1907.

U. S., Army, Judge Advocate General. *United States Military Reservations, National Cemeteries, and Military Parks* Edited by Lewis W. Call. Washington, DC: The Government Printing Office, 1910.

U. S., Army, Judge Advocate General. *United States Military Reservations, National Cemeteries, and Military Parks* Washington, DC: The Government Printing Office, 1916.

U. S., Army War College, Historical Section. *Order of Battle of the United States Land Forces in the World War (1917-19): Zone of Interior.* Washington, DC: The Government Printing Office, 1949.

U.S., Congress, House of Representatives. *Establish A National Military Park at Fort Stevens, House of Representatives Report No. 1537*, 68th Congress, 2d Session (February 20, 1925) (to accompany H.R. 11365).

U.S., Congress, House of Representatives. *House Executive Document No. 361*, 81st Congress, 1st Session, "Supplemental Estimate of Appropriation for the Department of the Interior," October 11, 1949.

U.S., Congress, House of Representatives. *Investigations Into the Affairs of the District of Columbia, House Report No. 72*, 42nd Congress, 2d Session (Serial 1542). Washington, DC: The Government Printing Office, 1872..

U.S., Congress, House of Representatives. *Journal of the House of Representatives of the United States . . .*, 57th Congress, 1st Session, 1901-02. Washington, DC: The Government Printing Office, 1902, 290 (HR 10528).

U.S., Congress, House of Representatives. *Journal of the House of Representatives of the United States . . .*, 58th Congress, 2d Session. Washington, DC: The Government Printing Office, 1904, 270 (HR 12149).

U.S., Congress, House of Representatives. *Journal of the House of Representatives of the United States . . .*, 58th Congress, 3d session, 1904-05. Washington, DC: The Government Printing Office, 1905, 455 (HR19204).

U.S., Congress, House of Representatives. *Journal of the House of Representatives of the United States . . .*, 1907-08, 60th Congress, 1st Session. Washington, DC: The Government Printing Office, 1908, 16, (HR291).

U.S., Congress, House of Representatives. *Journal of the House of Representatives of the United States . . .*, 66th Congress, 1st Session. Washington, DC: The Government Printing Office, 1919, 594 (HR 10695).

U.S., Congress, House of Representatives. *Journal of the House of Representatives of the United States . . .*, 67th Congress, 1st Session. Washington, DC: The Government Printing Office, 1921, 497 (HR 8792).

U.S., Congress, House of Representatives. *Journal of the House of Representatives of the United States . . .*, 67th Congress, 2d Session, 19221-22. Washington, DC: The Government Printing Office, 1922, 116 (HR 8792).

U.S., Congress, House of Representatives. *Journal of the House of Representatives of the United States . . .*, 68th Congress, 2d Session, 1924-25. Washington, DC: The Government Printing Office, 1924, 280, 288, 476 (S J.117).

U.S., Congress, House of Representatives. *Journal of the House of Representatives of the United States . . .*, 69th Congress, 1st session 1925-26. Washington, DC: The Government Printing Office, 1926, 739, 1099 (HR 12644).

U.S., Congress, House of Representatives. *Journal of the House of Representatives of the United States . . .*, 70th Congress, 1st Session, 1927-28. Washington, DC: The Government Printing Office, 1928, 378,

11744 (HR10556).

U.S., Congress, House of Representatives. *Journal of the House of Representatives of the United States* . 71st Congress, 2d session, 1929-30. Washington, DC: The Government Printing Office, 1930, 431, 523 (HR11489).

U. S., Congress, House of Representatives. *Military and Naval Defenses, House Executive Document No. 92*, 37th Congress, 2nd Session, 1862.

U. S., Congress, House of Representatives, Committee on Military Affairs. *Permanent Fortifications and Sea-Coast Defenses, House Report No. 86*, 37th Congress, 2nd Session, 1862.

U. S., Congress, Joint Committee on the Conduct of the War. *Report*. 6 Volumes and Supplement. Washington, D.C.: The Government Printing Office, 1863, 1865-66.

U.S., Congress, Senate. *Fort Stevens-Lincoln National Military Park; Senate Document No. 433*, 57th Congress, 1st Session, June 26, 1902.

U.S., Congress, Senate. *The Improvement of the Park System of the District of Columbia*; 57th Congress, 1st Session, *Senate Report No. 166*. Edited by Charles Moore. Washington, DC: The Government Printing Office, 1902.

U.S., Congress, Senate. *Journal of the Senate of the United States*, 56th Congress, 2d Session. Washington, DC: The Government Printing Office, 1901, 247 (S6065).

U.S., Congress, Senate. *Journal of the Senate of the United States*, 57th Congress, 1st Session, 1901-02. Washington, DC: The Government Printing Office, 1902, 228, 521, 527 (S4476).

U.S., Congress, Senate. *Journal of the Senate of the United States*, 58th Congress, 2d Session. Washington, DC: The Government Printing Office, 1904, 119 (S3886).

U.S., Congress, Senate. *Journal of the Senate of the United States*, 59th Congress, 1st Session, 1905-06. Washington, DC: The Government Printing Office, 1906, 525, 547 (S6265).

U.S., Congress, Senate. *Journal of the Senate of the United States*, 59th Congress, 2d Session. Washington, DC: The Government Printing Office, 1907, 91 (S7646).

U.S., Congress, Senate. *Journal of the Senate of the United States*, 60th Congress, 1st Session. Washington, DC: The Government Printing Office, 1908, 216 (S5132).

U.S., Congress, Senate. *Journal of the Senate of the United States*, 62 Congress, 2d Session. Washington, DC: The Government Printing Office, 1912, 75, 93, 107.

U.S., Congress, Senate. *Journal of the Senate of the United States . . .*, 62d Congress, 3rd Session. Washington, DC: The Government Printing Office, 1912, 70 (S8142).

U.S., Congress, Senate. *Journal of the Senate of the United States . . .*, 67th Congress, 1st Session. Washington, DC: The Government Printing Office, 1922, 14 (S4).

U.S., Congress, Senate. *Journal of the Senate of the United States . . .*, 68th Congress, 1st Session, 1923-24. Washington, DC: The Government Printing Office, 1924, 58 (S1340).

U.S., Congress, Senate. *Journal of the Senate of the United States . . .*, 68th Congress, 2d Session, 1924-25. Washington, DC: The Government Printing Office, 1925, 50 (S1340).

U.S., Congress, Senate. *Journal of the Senate of the United States . . .*, 69th Congress, 1st Session. Washington, DC: The Government Printing Office, 1926, 436, 712 (S4401).

U.S., Congress, Senate, Committee on the District of Columbia. *Park Improvement Papers: A Series of Twenty Papers Relating to the Improvement of Park System of the District of Columbia.* Washington, D.C.: The Government Printing Office, 1903.

U.S., Congress, Senate, Committee on the District of Columbia. *Park Improvement Papers: A Series of Twenty Papers Relating to the Improvement of Park System of the District of Columbia, No. 4, Fort Stevens, Where Lincoln Was Under Fire* by William V. Cox . Washington, D.C.: The Government Printing Office, 1903,17-25.

U. S., Corps of Engineers. *Regulations for the Corps of Engineers and Topographical Engineers.* Washington, DC: A.0.P. Nicholson, 1857.

U.S., Department of the Interior, National Park Service. *Fort Circle Parks Master Plan.* April 1968. Washington, DC: National Park Service, 1968.

U.S., Department of the Interior, National Park Service. *Guide Leaflet for the Tour of—Historic Civil War Defenses—Washington, D.C.* Sheet #1. Washington, DC: National Park Service, 1938.

U. S., Department of the Interior, National Park Service. *National Capital Parks.* Washington, D.C.: The Government Printing Office, 1963.

U. S., Department of the Interior, National Park Service, Cultural Resources, Park Historic Architecture Division. *Earthworks Landscape Management Manual.* Prepared Andropogon Associates, Ltd., Ecological Planning and Design. Washington, DC: The Government Printing Office, 1989.

U.S., Department of the Interior, National Park Service, George Washington Memorial Parkway. *Earthworks Landscape Management Plan. Fort Marcy*. Washington, DC: U.S., Department of the Interior, National Park Service, George Washington Memorial Parkway, 1995.

U. S., Engineer School. *Engineer Operations in Past Wars*. 2 Parts. Fort Humphreys, VA: Engineer School, 1926.

U. S., Engineer School. *History and Traditions of the Corps of Engineers' Engineer School ROTC Text ST25-1*. Fort Belvoir' VA: Engineer School, 1953.

U.S., Engineer School. *Pamphlet on the Evolution of the Art of Fortification, Engineer School Occasional Paper No. 58*. Prepared Under the Direction of William M. Black. Washington, DC: The Government Printing Office, 1919.

U. S., Inspector General's Office, *Outline Descriptions of the Posts and Stations of Troops in the Geographical Divisions and Departments of the United States*. Washington, DC: The Government Printing Office, 187).

U.S., Army, Judge Advocate General, *United States Military Reservations, National Cemeteries, and Military Parks*, Edited by Lewis W. Call. Washington, D.C.: The Government Printing Office, 1910.

U.S., Military Academy, West Point, Department of Military Art and Engineering. *Notes on Permanent Land Fortifications*. West Point, New York: Department of Military Art and Engineering, U.S. Military Academy, 1944. 18 pp. & 12 Figures.

U.S., National Archives. *Civil War Maps in the National Archives*. Washington, DC: The Government Printing Office, 1964.

U. S., National Archives. *A Guide to Civil War Maps in the National Archives*. Washington, DC: The Government Printing Office, 1986.

U. S., National Archives. *The Southeast During the Civil War: Selected Records in the National Archives of the United States, Reference Paper No. 69*. By Dale E. Floyd. Washington, DC: National Archives and Records Service, 1973.

U.S., National Capital Parks and Planning Commission. *Plans and Studies: Washington and Vicinity, National Capital Parks and Planning Commission Supplemental Technical Data, 1928*. Washington, DC: The Government Printing Office, 1929.

U.S., National Capital Planning Commission. *Fort Park System: A Re-evaluation Study of Fort Drive, Washington, D.C.* April 1965. By Fred W. Tuemmler and Associates, College Park, Maryland. Washington, DC: National Capital Planning Commission, 1965.

U.S., National Capital Planning Commission. *Planning Washington 1924-1976: An Era of Planning for the National Capital and Environs.* By Frederick Gutheim assisted by Toni Lee. Washington, DC: Smithsonian Institution Press, 1977.

U.S., National Capital Planning Commission. *Worthy of the Nation: The History of Planning for the National Capital.* Frederick Gutheim, Consultant. Washington, DC: Smithsonian Institution Press, 1977.

U.S., The National Commission on Fine Arts. *Tenth Report July 1, 1921—December 31, 1925.* Washington, DC: The Government Printing Office, 1926.

U.S., National Park Service, National Capital Parks. *Interpretive Prospectus. Fort Circle Parks. National Capital Parks. Washington, DC.* Washington, DC: The Government Printing Office, 1971.

U.S., National Park Service, National Capital Region. *Close To Home.* Washington, DC: The Government Printing Office, 1979.

U. S., Naval History Division. *Civil War Naval Chronology, 1861-1865.* Washington, DC: The Government Printing Office, 1971.

U. S., Navy Department. *Official Records of the Union and Confederate Navies in the War of the Rebellion.* Multivolumes. Washington, DC: The Government Printing Office, 1894-1927.

U. S., Office of National Capital Parks. *The Defenses of Washington, 1861-1865.* By Stanley W. McClure. Washington, DC: National Park Service, 1967.

U.S., Office of National Capital Parks, "A History of National Capital Parks, "By Cornelius W. Heine. Washington, DC: National Capital Parks, National Park Service, 1953.

U. S., Quartermaster Department, *Outline Description of U. S. Military Posts and Stations in the Year 1871.* Washington, DC: The Government Printing Office, 1872.

U.S., Surgeon's General's Office. *Surgeon General Circular No. 8, A Report on the Hygiene of the United States Army, with Descriptions of Military Posts.* Washington, DC: GPO, 1875.

U. S., Treasury Department. . . . *Statement of Appropriations and Expenditures for Public Buildings, Rivers and Harbors, Forts, Arsenals, Armories and Other Public Works from March 4, 1789, to June 30, 1882.* Washington, DC: The Government Printing Office, 1882.

U. S., War Department. *Annual Reports of the Secretary of War.* Washington, DC; Various Publishers, 1823-.

U. S., War Department. *Atlas to Accompany the Official Records of the Union and Confederate Armies.* 3 Volumes. Washington, DC: The Government Printing Office, 1891-95.

U. S., War Department, *Military Reservations.* Washington, DC: The Government Printing Office, 1937-42.

U.S., War Department. *Report of the Secretary of War, Being Part of the Message and Documents Communicated to the Two Houses of Congress at the Beginning of the Second Session of the Forty-Second Congress., House Executive Document 1,* Part 2, 42d Congress, 2d Session. Volume II. Washington, DC: The Government Printing Office, 1871.

U.S., War Department. *Report of the Secretary of War, with the Reports of Officers, for the Year 1869,* Accompanying Papers Abridged. Washington, DC: The Government Printing Office, 1869.

\U.S., War Department. *The War of the Rebellion: A Compilation of the Official Records of the Union and Confederate Armies.* 70 Volumes. Washington, DC: The Government Printing Office, 1880-1901.

U.S., Work Projects Administration, Federal Writer's Program. *Washington, D.C.: A Guide to the Nation' Capital, American Guide Series,* Randall Bond Truett, Editor, New Revised Edition (Original edition published by The George Washington University of Washington, D. C. In 1942) New York: Hastings House Publishers, 1968.

Vandiver, Frank E. *Jubal's Raid: General Early's Famous Attack on Washington in 1864.* New York: McGraw-Hill Book Company, Inc., 1960.

Vauban, Sebastien le Prestre de. *A Manual of Siegecraft and Fortification.* Translated and Edited by George A. Rothrock. Ann Arbor, MI: University of Michigan Press, 1968.

Verill, G.W. "Defenses of Washington Fort Scott; Sabbath at Ft. Scott (Letter of soldier G.W. Verill, November 30, 1862)." *The Arlington Historical Magazine,* 6, October 1979, 13-14.

Viele, Egbert L. "Field Fortifications." Chapter IX in Egbert L. Viele. *Hand-book for Active Service; Containing Practical Instructions in Campaign Duties, for the Use of Volunteers.* New York: D. Van Nostrand, 1861, 92-148.

Vorek, Robert. "A Preliminary Report of the 1984 Excavations at Fort Reno Park, Washington, D. C."

Wagner, Arthur L. "Hasty Entrenchments in the War of Secession." In The Military Historical Society of Massachusetts. *Civil and Mexican Wars 1861, 1846.* Volume 13 of the *Papers of the Military Historical Society of Massachusetts.* Boston: The Military Historical Society of Massachusetts, 1913, 127-53.

Wagner, Arthur L. "Hasty Entrenchments in the War of Secession." *Journal of the Military Service Institution of the United States,* 22, February 1898, 225-46.

A Walking Tour of Fort C.F. Smith Park. Pamphlet for Arlington Park. Arlington, VA: Arlington, n.d.

Walton, Thomas. "The 1901 McMillan Commission: Beaux Arts Plan for the Nation's Capital." Ph.D. dissertation, Catholic University, 1980.

Warrington, J. Les. "In Defense of Washington." *AA World* (Potomac Dir.), 3, May/June 1983, 2f.

Washington, D.C., Neighborhood Planning Councils 2 and 3. *Footsteps: Historical Walking tours of Chevy Chase, Cleveland Park, Tenleytown, Friendship.* Washington, DC: Neighborhood Planning Councils 2 and 3, 1976.

Washington During War Time: A Series of Papers Showing the Military, Political, and Social Phases During 1861 to 1865. Official Souvenir of the Thirty-Sixth Annual Encampment of the Grand Army of the Republic. Collected and Edited by Marcus Benjamin Under the Direction of the Committee on Literature for the Encampment. Washington, DC: The National Tribune Co., n.d.

Ways, Henry C. *The Washington Aqueduct 1852-1992.* Washington, D.C.: The Government Printing Office, 1996(?).

Webb, Anne C. "Fort Strong on Arlington Heights." *The Arlington Historical Magazine,* 5, October 1973, 34-39.

Webb, Anne Ciprani. "Fort Strong on Arlington Heights," *Periodical: The Journal of the Council on Abandoned Military Posts,* 4, July 1972, 2-6.

Wert, Jeffry E. "The Snicker Gap War," *Civil War Times Illustrated,* 17, July 1978, 30-40.

Wheatley, William J. "Fort DeRussy to be Restored: Surrounding Section in Rock Creek Park Being Cleared to Open Area," *The Washington Star,* Dec. 5, 1926;

White, Jean M. "Access Road Will Be Built to Fort Marcy," *The Washington Post,* Nov 6, 1960.

White, John C. "A Review of the Services of the Regular Army During the Civil War (Engineers)." *Journal of the Military Service Institution of the United States,* 45, September-October 1909, 226-29.

White, Thomas E. "Washington and Environs— 1865." *Arlington Historical Magazine*, 3, October 1968, 17-20.

Whitehorne, Joseph W.A. *The Battle of Second Manassas: Self-Guided Tour.* Washington, DC: The Government Printing Office, 1990.

Whitt, Jane Chapman. *Elephants and Quakert Guns: A History of Civil War and Circus Days.* New York: Vantage Press, Inc., 1966.

Whyte, James H. *The Uncivil War: Washington during the Reconstruction 1865-78.* New York: Twayne Publishers, 1958.

Willett, James R. "A Method of Determining a Plane of Defilement." *United States Service Magazine*, 1, June 1864, 618-21.

Williams, Ames W. "The Location of Battery Rodgers." *Echoes of History*, 5, April 1975, 33-34.

Williams, Eilliam Hazaiah. "The Negro in the District of Columbia during Reconstruction." *The Howard (University) Review*, 1, June 1924, 97-148.

Williams, J.C. *Life in Camp.* New Hampshire: Claremont Manufacturing Co., 1884.

Williams, Melvin Roscoe. "Blacks in Washington, D.C., 1860-1870." Ph.D. dissertation, The Johns Hopkins University, 1976.

Williams, Melvin Roscoe. "A Blueprint for Change: The Black Community in Washington, D.C., 1860-1870." *Columbia Historical Society Records*, Vols. 71-72, 1971-72, 358-93.

Williams, William Hazaiah. "The Negro in the District of Columbia During Reconstruction." M.A. thesis, Howard University, 1924.

Wills, Mary A. *Confederate Batteries Along the Potomac.* Commissioned by the Prince William County Historical Commission, June, 1978. Reprinted, 1983.

Wills, Mary A. *The Confederate Blockade of Washington, D. C., 1861-1862.* Parsons, WV: McClain Printing Co., 1975.

Wilshin, Francis F. *Manassas (Bull Run) National Battlefield Park, Virginia.* Washington, DC: The Government Printing office, 1953.

Wilson, John M. "The Defenses of Washington, 1861-1865." #38 in The Washington, DC Commandery, The Military Order of the Loyal Legion of the United States. *War Papers*. Washington, DC: The Military Order of the Loyal Legion of the United States, 1901.

Wood, John E. "The Water Supply of Washington, D. C." *Military Engineer*, 16, July-August 1924, 316-19.

Woodruff, Thomas M. "Early War Days in the Nation's Capital." In Commandery of Minnesota, Military Order of the Loyal Legion of the United States. *Glimpses of the Nation's Struggle*. Volume 3. New York: Merrill, 1893, 87-105.

"World's Greatest Earthworks Protected Capital." *The Sunday Washington Star*, March 1, 1931, pages 1-2, 7.

Worthington, Glenn H. *Fighting For Time or the Battle that Saved Washington and Mayhap the Union*. Reprint. Shippensburg, PA: Beidel Publishing House, Inc., 1985.

Wright, David R. "Civil War Field Fortifications: An Analysis of Theory and Practical Application." M.A. thesis, Middle Tennessee State University, 1982.

Yost, Ann. "Off to the War: Backwar-r-r-d, March!" *The Washington Post*, July 4, 1986.

Young, John M. *Excavations at Fort Lincoln, Washington, D.C.* September 25, 1968.

Youngberg, Gilbert A. *History of Engineer Troops in the United States Army, 1775-1901, Engineer School Occasional Paper No. 37*. Washington, DC: Press of the Engineer School, 1910.

Yule, Henry. *Fortification for Officers of the Army and Students of Military History*. London: William Blackwood and Sons, 1851.

Zack Spratt, "Rock Creek Bridges," *Records of the Columbia Historical Society of Washington, D.C.*, 1953-56, Vols. 53-56, 107-08.